THE GAUNTLET
(EN HANSKE)

BY

BJÖRNSTJERNE BJÖRNSON

THE GAUNTLET
(EN HANSKE)

BY

BJÖRNSTJERNE BJÖRNSON

TRANSLATED FROM THE NORWEGIAN WITH AN INTRODUCTION BY

EDWIN BJÖRKMAN

Fredonia Books
Amsterdam, The Netherlands

The Gauntlet
(En Hanske)

by
Björnstjerne Björnson

ISBN: 1-4101-0360-9

Reprinted from the 1913 edition

Fredonia Books
Amsterdam, The Netherlands
http://www.fredoniabooks.com

In order to make original editions of historical works
available to scholars at an economical price, this
facsimile of the original edition of 1913 is
reproduced from the best available copy and has
been digitally enhanced to improve legibility, but the
text remains unaltered to retain historical
authenticity.

CONTENTS

INTRODUCTION

INTRODUCTION

BJÖRNSTJERNE BJÖRNSON was born December 8, 1832, in a solitary rectory, lost among the mountains of northern Norway. His father was then the spiritual head of the smallest parish in the whole country. There the boy spent the first years of his life, seeing more of nature than of man. When he was six the family removed to the Romsdal district, on the Atlantic coast, which is one of the most beautiful and also most characteristic parts of Norway. In 1843 the boy was sent to school in the little fishing-town of Molde, not far from his parental home, and at eighteen he went to Christiania to study at the same school where the young Ibsen was then preparing himself for entrance into the national university.

He was only twenty when he wrote his first play—historical, of course, with a theme from the Sagas. It was accepted by the Christiania Theatre, but before it reached a performance the young author realised its shortcomings and withdrew it. His public career began as dramatic critic on a daily newspaper, and in this capacity he made history by leading the opposition against the Danish influence, which had until then prevailed on the national stage. From the very first he spoke with the assurance and authority of a born chieftain, and however frequently challenged, his leadership was never surrendered or lost. Toward the Norway with which the world is familiar to-day—a nation having a culture marvellously disproportionate to its physical and economical conditions—no one man has contributed more than Björnson, and to understand his spirit is to understand the country itself.

His first dramatic work of lasting value was produced in 1856, after a visit to the Swedish city of Upsala, where students from the three Scandinavian countries had met for the promotion of mutual sympathy. It was a brief historic play named "Between the Battles," which, because of its novelty of form, exercised an unmistakable influence both on Ibsen and Strindberg. Its terse prose was that of the old Sagas. The next year Björnson produced and published his first peasant tale, "Synnöve Solbakken" (Synnöve Sunnyside). Henrik Jäger, the literary historian of Norway, says that two things assured the success of that tale and those that followed: their style, at once picturesque and simple; and their author's discovery that mental reserve and laconic expression are characteristic traits of the Norwegian peasant.

To this discovery and to his own charming application of it, Björnson was led by a double study: of the old Sagas and of the peasants themselves. Always and everywhere he strove to recognise the unbroken connection between the life of the past and the life still led by the people around him. The result of his effort was that he forestalled Maeterlinck in effective use of commonplace, almost meaningless words.

In 1857 he succeeded Ibsen as leader of the theatre started at Bergen by Ole Bull, and during the eighteen months he remained in that place he married a young actress, Caroline Reimers, whose devotion and loving comprehension of his genius served him as a valuable support to the very end of his life. On the whole, the fate of Björnson was always fortunate, and not the least so in regard to his marriage. It resulted in a relationship that coloured his art, and made him logically what he later became: a champion of the new womanhood. And few have done more than he to assert and defend the essential equality of the two sexes.

After his return to Christiania in 1859, he wrote a number of charming lyrics, many of which were set to music by Half-dan Kjerulf, who was then Norway's greatest composer. He wrote also several patriotic songs, and one of these, "Yea, We Love the Land that Bore Us," caught the popular taste to such an extent that it rapidly won acceptance as the national hymn.

Björnson was the first man in Norway to receive an annual pension from the government. This happened in 1863, when he was only thirty-one years old, and in the same year he de-livered the first of those public lectures which came to form such an important part of his activity, bringing him into a personal contact with the people that a man like Ibsen could never attain. As a speaker he exercised a magnetism that has rarely been equalled either in his own country or outside of it. Yet his words were simple enough, though at times he could rise to the highest poetic flights even when speaking im-promptu. But what really secured his hold on his listeners was his transparent sincerity, his earnestness, and his insist-ence on telling them not what they liked to hear, but what he believed to be right and true. Add to this that he possessed an almost uncanny perception of what was going on in the mind of the people, and that he knew well how to reckon with what he thus perceived, although often enough his task was to lead his countrymen to a position diametrically op-posed to the one previously held by them.

In 1862 Björnson wrote his first really significant play, the trilogy "Sigurd the Bad," which two years later was followed by another fine, although not epoch-making piece of work, the historical drama "Mary Stuart in Scotland." When, in 1865, he broke new ground at last, the medium he used for the purpose was slight enough: a two-act play named "The Newly Married Couple." But it was a prose play dealing with the everyday life of his own time and place. It displayed no violent passions, and was in no way sensational. All it did was to portray "the soul processes taking place within a young woman as she leaves her parents' home to follow her husband—that is, as she ceases to be primarily a daughter, in order to become primarily a wife."

In spite of its unmistakable shortcomings, the play exercised a wide influence, and not the least so on Ibsen, who a few years later produced "The League of Youth." The relationship between Ibsen and Björnson, which always remained one of mutual give and take even when they were emotionally estranged, has often been represented as one of a smaller mind to a greater. The truth is that Björnson was as great as Ibsen, but in a different way. The latter specialised in the drama, while the former was always tempted to embrace the entire field of literary endeavour; nay, the whole vast realm of human life in all its varied manifestations.

Ibsen became in the end one of the world's great dramatists, and one of the corner-stones of the new drama which is only now coming into existence. If we restrict the comparison between them to this field alone, Björnson must necessarily suffer, but even then a closer analysis will prove him to have rendered much greater service than is generally admitted. The constant exchange of impulses and ideas between him and Ibsen constitutes one of the most interesting phenomena recorded in literary history, and, strange as it may seem, in this mutual exchange it was Björnson who gave the most. As a rule it seems as if the seeds of the forms still to be developed sprang into being within his richer and more enthusiastic mind, to be later nursed into perfection within the colder but more persistent mind of Ibsen. The evolution of the man who wrote "Rosmersholm" may be characterised as a process of slow and painful elimination, while the onward march of Björnson was one of triumphant discovery. Three times, in particular, the latter seems to have furnished the "clue" needed by Ibsen in his tormenting pursuit of self-knowledge. This Björnson did through two of the plays already mentioned, "Between the Battles" and "The Newly Married Couple," and through a third one that followed in 1875, "A Business Failure."

Nor does this reflected importance of Björnson, derived from his influence on the development of his more famous rival, dispose of his significance in the annals of the modern drama. Some of his plays belong to the greatest produced during the last century, and will undoubtedly live for a long time to come. They are less universal in their application than those of Ibsen, but they are also more human, better adapted to that side of man which forbids his living up to his highest possibilities at each single moment of his life. I do not mean to say that Björnson's dramatic art administers to the weaknesses of man, as do so many plays of ephemeral attraction; it simply reckons with them. Somebody said once that whenever Björnson had thundered for a while, he had to smile a little—and his smile was not grim like that of Ibsen. In other words, his work is more emotional than that of Ibsen, and for this very reason it should exert an increasing appeal on the generation that is now arriving at maturity.

"The Editor," a drama picturing the demoralising effect exercised by an influential press under the leadership of selfish and unscrupulous men, preceded "A Business Failure," but though belonging to the new order, it was still too uncertain in form, and too polemical in spirit, to achieve the revolution resulting from the later play. "A Business Failure" was not only the first wholly successful specimen of the modern prose play produced in the Scandinavian North, but it served also to introduce money and business into Scandinavian literature, and thence into the literature of Germany. In this respect it went beyond what had already been achieved by Augier and the younger Dumas in France. To them love was always the supreme theme; to Björnson it was only one strand out of many that are woven into the rope of life. For this very reason, perhaps, "A Business Failure" achieved an additional distinction, which by many critics has been declared its greatest: namely that of being the first true stage picture of a Norwegian home. And this quality of domestic realism goes far to explain why it became at once, and has always remained, a great favourite in Germany, while to this day it has failed to win approval in France.

In 1877 Björnson published his first novel, "Magnhild," which, while an exquisite piece of work, was rendered significant chiefly by the new view of marriage voiced in it. If not based on love, Björnson dared to assert—and the assertion was a very radical one in those days—marriage was as immoral as any illegitimate relationship, if not worse, and the breaking of it must be held not only permissible, but a duty. In other ways, too, the novel was a forerunner of the play, "The Gauntlet," by which, a few years later, Björnson furnished one of the main impulses for the Scandinavian feminist movement.

Of "The New System," completed in 1879, Björnson said himself that its interest was psychological rather than dramatic. For this very reason, however, it should be germane to the present time. And it derives still further interest from being the main dramatic expression of the principle which had gradually become Björnson's final formulation of man's foremost duty to himself, to others, and to life in its entirety.

The cry uttered by Ibsen in "Brand" as the utmost wisdom
to be distilled out of life was: "Be yourself!" The cry of
Björnson, uttered first in an address to the students of Christiania University, and later made the ever-present under-
current in "The New System," was "Live in Truth!" What
he meant was that no appearances matter in the end; that
nothing really counts but what we *are;* and that, conse-
quently, the way to perfection lies through a frank acknowl-
edgment of our innermost natures. And this demand for
truthfulness he extended to the state as well as to the individual. In these days, when the best men all over the
civilised world seem agreed that the most effective remedy
for social evils and mistakes lies in publicity, "The New
System" has a timeliness almost equalling that of a political
platform.

The electoral campaign of 1879, which placed the Radical
party, known as the "Left," in control of the government,
marked a turning point in the country's history as well as
one of the first definite steps toward the dissolution of the
union with Sweden. Björnson was the soul of the movement which carried that campaign to victory, thus extending
his leadership also to the field of politics. How powerful that
leadership was may be judged from the nickname given him
of "Norway's uncrowned king." Both in Sweden and
among his opponents in Norway, it was often asserted that
he used his position in a manner meant to enhance his own
fame and power. But although, like all strong and far-
seeing men, he was arbitrary in his self-assertion, yet his mo-
tives remained always pure and his purposes raised far above
those of men usually classed as politicians. And in all he
did to guide his country to self-consciousness and spiritual as
well as political independence, there seems to have been little,
if anything, of hatred toward those that stood in the way.

It was for those that made life small and mean and ugly that his actual hatred was reserved, and it never was more likely to break into open flame than when anybody repeated the time-honoured belief that life was impelled by desires rather than by duties. The presence and power of such desires, especially those connected with man's sexual life, he admitted readily, and he was always prepared to take them into practical account. But that any desire must needs be stronger than the man within whom it makes itself felt, he neither could nor would admit. Out of this feeling on his part sprang "The Gauntlet" first of all, and later the novel "The House of the Kurts." The main objective of his attack was the so-called double standard of morality, by which a separate code of sexual ethics was provided for each of the two sexes. It was by no means the first time that standard had been attacked, but until then its enemies had almost invariably been satisfied to demand for woman the liberties accorded to man by time-honoured custom. Björnson was probably the first one to assert—and undoubtedly the very first one to do so in a work of high artistic quality—that men must be as chaste as women if they are to retain that precious stamp of social approval known as "respectability." Other writers had defended the woman "with a past"; Björnson dared to attack the man with a similar past—and for a time, at least, he did so with undoubted success. Whether his position will finally be assumed by the race in this matter remains yet to be seen, but as long as the race continues the discussion of that matter, with all its ramifications among human institutions and ideas, Björnson's play must be counted a contribution that cannot be overlooked by any seeker after truth.

Before he was led to take this extreme attitude in questions of sexual relationship, his spiritual position had in other ways undergone a marked and far-reaching change. From his parents he had inherited not only a strong religious feeling, but a view of Christianity that rendered it a satisfactory outlet for a typical Scandinavian tendency, designated by one of the younger Swedish writers as "the passion for the infinite." During the seventies Björnson drifted more and more away from his inherited attitude, led principally by the evolutionary re-interpretations of scientific truths. In 1880–81 he made a lecture trip to the United States, which seems also to have, in many ways, furthered and hastened this broadening of his spirit. Shortly after his return he published a story named "Dust," in which his new attitude of mind found its first artistic expression. It was his "Ghosts"; but the inheritance from which he saw men suffering was spiritual rather than physical.

This change within him found its clearest and yet fairest utterance in the first part of "Beyond Our Power," published the same year as "The Gauntlet." In "Dust" he had taken issue against outgrown religious ideas. In the play he turned once for all against man's craving to escape from life's realities by building up around himself a supernatural sham-existence. He had come to feel that the belief in miracles lay at the bottom of the Christian faith, its most typical characteristic, and he had also come to feel that this belief implied an unrealisable hope of a special setting aside of universal laws for the benefit of the individual who did not dare to face the consequences of his own acts.

In a second play, named also "Beyond Our Power"—which is a sequel to the earlier one, but written in such a manner that the two plays remain mutually independent—there appears a character named *Johan Sverd*, and a blind man might see that he is none but Björnson himself. In his mouth Björnson has laid a passage that explains not only what moved him to write the two parts of "Beyond Our Power," but also the spirit that informed his entire subsequent artistic activity.

"But I tell you," says *Johan Sverd*, "that the day will come when mankind must discover that there lies more greatness and poetry in what is natural and possible—however insignificant it may frequently appear—than in the world's whole store of supernaturalism, from the first sun-myth down to the latest sermon preached about it."

In his later development, Björnson was almost Greek in his aversion to what pretended to exceed human measures while still having its roots within man himself. "Is there anything more gruesome," cries another character in the play just mentioned, "than that force within ourselves which goads us on to what our whole nature resists? And can happiness be possible on this earth until our reason becomes so completely a part of our nature, that nothing retains the power of using us in that way?"

Björnson never wrote more than one novel of the length to which American and English readers have been accustomed. It appeared in 1884, and the name of it, literally translated, is "The Flags Are Flying." In English it is generally known as "The House of the Kurts." The problem which its author set for himself in this story was that of heredity *vs.* education—and it was strictly in keeping with his life-long optimism that he found a verdict for education, by which he believed it possible to overcome the tendencies implanted in the organism at birth. At the same time, however, Björnson returned in this book once more to the question of sexual morality, but less with a view to stating what it ought to imply, than with a hope of outlining a road for the attainment of it. Here as elsewhere, his plea was for knowledge as the one firm basis on which life may be safely rested. For

the innocence that is based on ignorance he showed not only
contempt but actual hostility.

His greatest novel was undoubtedly "In the Ways of God,"
printed in 1889. There science and religion, knowledge and
faith, the natural and the supernatural stand face to face in
the persons of a physician and a clergyman. The entire
book, from the first line to the last, is a sermon against intol-
erance, but clothed in exquisitely artistic form. Life comes
first, religion and everything else in the second place, is its
lesson. God is still supreme in this new world of Björnson's,
but it is a God of law and evolution, not of lawless miracles.
And what the author has to say against the superstitions and
the dogmas commonly masquerading under the name of religion may as well be said against the dead and stiffened
dogmas of a science believing itself to have said the final
word on life and its limitless possibilities.

The second part of "Beyond Our Power," published in
1895, did for social superstition what the earlier play had done
for that element in religion which Björnson had come to regard as lying "beyond the limits of man." It is one of the
most powerful portrayals of the modern struggle between
capital and labour which western literature has produced so
far. At the same time, it presents a rarely beautiful picture
of love between brother and sister.

From 1898 to 1904 Björnson produced four plays, notable
both in spirit and form. All but one of them dealt with the
relationship between the coming and the going generations,
between parents and children. With sympathy for both, and
understanding of the new as well as the old, Björnson, as a
rule, took sides against the Nietzschean tendencies of the
younger generations. The last of those plays, "Dayland,"
was his "Fathers and Sons," but unlike Turgeniev's work, it
brings the two warring elements to a mutual understanding,

based on the fact that age, if willing to see, may recognise its own youth in the children, while these, as they grow older, tend to revert to the position still held by their elders. This play was dedicated to the Swedish Academy, from which Björnson in 1903 had received the Nobel prize for literature.

During his later years much of his time was devoted to efforts on behalf of two ideas in which he believed the future happiness of mankind principally involved. Those were the ideas of universal peace, and of the gradual federation of related races which, in the course of time, had become broken up into hostile nationalities. Dealing first of all with his own race, he advocated a Pan-Germanic ideal, based not on conquest, but on voluntary combination. At the same time he was tireless in his pleas for justice to oppressed racial groups, like those of the Poles and the Finlanders, the Danes of Schleswig-Holstein, and the Austrian Slovaks.

In 1909, within less than a year of his death, he brought out a final play, "When the Young Wine Blossoms," which proved an astounding revelation of powers retained to the very verge of the grave. In this last work, as in almost all its predecessors, Björnson displayed a good humour that literally sparkled. Reformer and prophet that he was, he was nevertheless a man who saw more of life's pleasant than of its unpleasant sides. And most of the time there was a merry twinkle in his eye that sometimes expanded into an abandon more Gallic than Scandinavian. But his laughter was always as innocent as it was whole-hearted.

As the presentiment of approaching death seized him at last, he made a final endeavour to preserve the life he liked so well. Leaving his beloved homestead, Aulestad, he made his way to Paris, and there he lingered, now hopeful and now resigned, until the end came in 1910. First of all, and from first to last, he was a great personality—a man who towered so high that even his own work looks small in comparison with what he *was*. Clean, strong, fiery, gifted with a wonderful magnetic power, he seemed throughout his long life a giant among ordinary men. Rarely, if ever, has a private individual to such an extent been able to stamp himself on the life and fate of a nation. Still more rarely has such an individual so completely refrained from using his exceptional position for the promotion of his private interests. And it must be held rarest of all that a man thus favoured preserved to the end the simple virtues that are generally associated only with those lowly ones whose position removes them beyond the reach of temptation.

A CHRONOLOGICAL LIST OF PLAYS BY BJÖRNSTJERNE BJÖRNSON

THE GAUNTLET
(EN HANSKE)
1883

CHARACTERS

RIIS
MRS. RIIS
SVAVA, *their daughter*
CHRISTENSEN
MRS. CHRISTENSEN
ALF, *their son*
DR. NORDAN
KARL HOFF
MARGIT, *maid at the Riises'*
THOMAS, *the man-servant of Dr. Nordan*

THE GAUNTLET

(EN HANSKE)

ACT I

*A room with double doors in the middle of the rear wall. The
doors are open and show a park, through the trees of which
may be seen glimpses of the sea. There are windows on
both sides of the doorway. Both side walls also have doors.
Between the door on the right and the nearest window
toward the park stands a piano. Against the opposite wall
stands a cabinet. On either side, nearest the audience,
there is a sofa with a small table, easy-chairs and other
chairs in front of it.*

FIRST SCENE

MRS. RIIS. DR. NORDAN.

*MRS. RIIS is seated on the left-hand sofa. DR. NORDAN
is sitting on a chair right between the tables. His head
is covered with a straw hat which he has pushed far back
on his head. A large handkerchief lies across one knee.
He is leaning forward over his hands, which are resting
on the top of his walking stick.*

MRS. RIIS. Why, you are not listening to me at all.

NORDAN. What was it you asked?

MRS. RIIS. About the suit against Mrs. North—what else
could it have been?

NORDAN. The suit against Mrs. North! I had a talk with Christensen a few moments ago. He has advanced the money and will try to get the banks to stop the suit. But this I have told you before. What more do you want?

MRS. RIIS. The gossip, my dear friend, the gossip.

NORDAN. Oh, we men don't tell tales on each other as a rule.—Isn't it about time to let *him* know about it? [*Nodding toward the door on the right*] He's in there now, isn't he?

MRS. RIIS. Let us wait.

NORDAN. For Christensen must have his money back, of course. I have promised him that.

MRS. RIIS. Of course. I hope you never imagined anything else?

NORDAN. [*Rising*] Well, I am going away for a little rest, and now Christensen will have to look after that matter.—I suppose it was a grand affair last night?

MRS. RIIS. No pomp of any kind.

NORDAN. No, the Christensens never indulge in ostentation. But numbers made up for it, I suppose.

MRS. RIIS. I have never seen so many people at a private affair.

NORDAN. Is Svava up?

MRS. RIIS. She is out for a bath.

NORDAN. Already? Did you get home that early?

MRS. RIIS. Oh, about twelve, I think. Svava wanted to get home. Mr. Riis stayed much longer, I believe.

NORDAN. Hm—the card-tables!—She was radiant, I suppose?

MRS. RIIS. Why didn't you come?

NORDAN. I never attend engagement or wedding feasts. Never. The sacrificing of those wreathed and veiled victims —oh!

MRS. RIIS. But, dear doctor, don't you believe with all of us, that this will turn out a happy marriage?

NORDAN. He is a fine fellow. But nevertheless—I have been fooled so often— Uh, huh!

MRS. RIIS. But she was happy. And so she is to-day.

NORDAN. Well, it's too bad I can't see her. Good morning, madam.

MRS. RIIS. Good morning, my dear doctor. So you are going away now?

NORDAN. I have to have a breathing spell.

MRS. RIIS. Yes, you need it. Well, good luck to you— and I thank you with all my heart!

NORDAN. And I thank you, Mrs. Riis! [*As he walks out*] Too bad I couldn't say good-bye to Svava!

SECOND SCENE

MRS. RIIS. *Later* RIIS.

MRS. RIIS *takes a foreign periodical from the table at the left and makes herself comfortable on the sofa in such a position that she faces the park. During the next two scenes she reads as often as she has a chance.*

RIIS. [*Comes from the right; he is in his shirt sleeves and busily occupied with his collar*] Good morning!—Was that Nordan who left?

MRS. RIIS. Yes.

RIIS *goes toward the door on the left, turns and disappears through the door on the right; then he comes in again and performs the same manœuvre; all the time he is struggling with his collar.*

MRS. RIIS. Is there anything I can help you with?

Riis. Thanks just the same! These modern shirts are a nuisance. I bought a few in Paris.

Mrs. Riis. I think you brought home a whole dozen?

Riis. And a half! [*He goes into the room on the right, comes out again, makes the same excursion to the left as before, accompanied by the same struggle with the collar as before*] Otherwise I am speculating on something.

Mrs. Riis. It must be some very intricate question.

Riis. So it is.—So it is.—Indeed!—Well, if this collar isn't— There! At last! [*He disappears and returns again, but now with the collar in his hand*] I am thinking of—thinking of— of what our dear daughter is made up.

Mrs. Riis. Of what she is made up?

Riis. Yes—how much of you, and how much of me, and so on.—That is, what she has from your family, and what from mine, and so on.—Svava is a remarkable girl.

Mrs. Riis. She is, indeed.

Riis. As a whole, she is neither you nor me—nor the two of us together.

Mrs. Riis. Svava is something more.

Riis. And something considerably more at that. [*He disappears once more, whereupon he reappears with his coat on and engaged in brushing it off*] What did you say?

Mrs. Riis. Nothing.—For that matter, Svava takes more after my mother than after anybody else.

Riis. Well, I declare! Svava, with her quiet, graceful ways—what are you thinking of?

Mrs. Riis. Svava can be passionate, too.

Riis. Svava never neglects the outward forms as your mother did.

Mrs. Riis. You never understood my mother. But, of course, I admit that they differ in many things also.

RIIS. Tremendously!—Can you see now, that I was right when I began to talk all sorts of languages to her while she was still a mere slip of a girl? Do you see now? You used to object.

MRS. RIIS. I was against having her bothered with it all the time—and also against your constant jumping from one thing to another.

RIIS. But the results, my dear—the results?

[Humming to himself.

MRS. RIIS. I hope you don't mean to say that it is the languages that have made her what she is?

RIIS. [*As he disappears again*] Not the languages, but— [*From the other room*] The languages have done a lot. Did you notice her last night? She has *savoir vivre*, hasn't she?

[Coming out again.

MRS. RIIS. That isn't what one cares most for in Svava.

RIIS. Oh, no.—On board the steamer somebody asked me if I were related to the Miss Riis who had started the kindergarten movement in this city. I replied that I had the honour of being her father. Then you should have seen the man. Why, it actually gave me a lump in the throat.

MRS. RIIS. Yes, the kindergartens have been a success from the very first.

RIIS. And I suppose they brought about her engagement also—did they?

MRS. RIIS. You had better ask her.

RIIS. But you don't notice my clothes at all.

MRS. RIIS. Oh, yes, I do.

RIIS. And not so much as a teeny-weeny gasp of admiration? At such a general effect—such a combination of colours —down to the very shoes—the handkerchief even? What do you say?

MRS. RIIS. How old are you, dear?

Riis. Oh, keep quiet! But for that matter—how old do you think I am taken for?

Mrs. Riis. About forty, of course.

Riis. "Of course,"—how genuine that sounds from your lips! But this dress is a sort of triumphal overture, composed at Cologne on receipt of the telegram about Svava's engagement. Think only: at Cologne, a mere ten-hour ride from Paris. But I couldn't wait ten hours—to such an extent was my sense of personal elegance increased by the thought of becoming related by marriage to the richest family in the country.

Mrs. Riis. And did it stop at that one suit?

Riis. What a question! Wait only till my trunks come out of the custom-house.

Mrs. Riis. Yes, then we are in for it, I suppose.

Riis. Are you in for it? Why, think of it—an overjoyed papa who, at the crucial moment, happens to find himself at Paris——

Mrs. Riis. And what did you think then of the party yesterday?

Riis. I thought it a fortunate chance that the steamer was delayed so that I was dropped down, as if by magic, right in the midst of a *fête champêtre*. And one given in honour of the dear daughter, at that, where, of course, papa found himself more than welcome!

Mrs. Riis. What time did you get home last night?

Riis. Do you think we could escape playing cards even yesterday? It was impossible to refuse, for I was asked to sit at table with Abraham, Isaac, and Jacob—that is, with our host, the Prime Minister, and old man Holk. It was an immense honour to be permitted to lose one's money to such bigwigs. And I lose always, as you know.—I came home about three, I should say.—What is it you are reading?

MRS. RIIS. The *Fortnightly*.

RIIS. Has there been anything good in it while I was away?
[*He begins to hum a melody*.

MRS. RIIS. Ye-es.—Here is something about heredity now, that you ought to read. It fits in with what we started to talk of.

RIIS. Do you know that melody? [*He hurries over to the piano*] It's all the go just now. I heard it all over Germany. [*Begins to play and sing, but breaks off abruptly*] Let me get the music, while I have it in mind!

> *He goes into the room at the right and returns with a sheet of music; sits down at the piano again and begins to sing and play as before.*

THIRD SCENE

> MRS. RIIS. RIIS. SVAVA *enters through the door on the left*.

RIIS. [*Looks around, stops, and jumps up*] Good morning, my dear! Good morning! I have hardly had a chance to speak to you yet. At the party last night everybody was taking you away from me.
[*He kisses her and leads her down the stage*.

SVAVA. Well, why were you so slow in coming home?

RIIS. Why didn't some people give notice when they intended to become engaged?

SVAVA. Because those people didn't know anything about it until it had already happened. Good morning again, mother dear!   [*She kneels down beside her mother*.

MRS. RIIS. Oh, what a smell of out of doors there is about you! Have you been walking in the woods after your bath?

SVAVA. [*Rising to her feet*] Yes, and just as I was coming

home, Alf passed by and waved a greeting up to me. He
will be here in a minute.

RIIS. To tell the truth—and one should always tell the
truth—I had quite given up the hope of seeing our old maid
so happy.

SVAVA. Yes, indeed! I had quite lost hope myself.

RIIS. Until the prince arrived.

SVAVA. Until the prince arrived—who had taken his time
in coming.

RIIS. And for whom you had been waiting for ever and a
day?

SVAVA. Not at all. I had never even given him a thought.

RIIS. This is becoming mysterious.

SVAVA. It is a mystery how two people who have known
each other since childhood without ever giving a thought to
each other, all of a sudden—for that's the way it happened.
Beginning with a certain given moment he became in my eyes
quite a different man.

RIIS. While in the eyes of all the rest he remained the same
as before.

SVAVA. I hope so!

RIIS. At least he has become a little less solemn—in my
eyes.

SVAVA. Yes, I saw you two laughing together last night.
What was it about?

RIIS. We were talking of the best manner of making one's
way through this world of ours. And I presented him with
my renowned three principles of life.

MRS. RIIS *and* SVAVA. Already!

RIIS. They made quite a hit with him. Do you recall
them, irreverent child that you are?

SVAVA. No. 1: never disgrace yourself.

RIIS. No. 2: never incommode anybody else.

Svava. No. 3: always be in fashion.—They are not *very* difficult to recall, seeing that they are neither deep nor dark.

Riis. But all the harder to put into practice! And that's just the merit of all such principles.—Accept my compliments on your new morning dress. Everything considered, it is really "sweet."

Svava. Everything considered—that means, considering that you did not help to select it.

Riis. Yes, for *I* should never have chosen those trimmings for it—but "everything considered," it might be worse. And the cut—hm—yes?—Well, now you just wait till my trunks get here.

Svava. Surprises?

Riis. Great ones!—And I have something for you at once.
[*Goes out.*

Svava. I think he is more restless than ever, mamma.

Mrs. Riis. It's the joy of it, girl!

Svava. And yet there is always something suppressed about papa's restlessness. He is— [Riis *returns from the right*] Do you know what the Prime Minister said of you yesterday?

Riis. Oh, well, a gentleman of that kind has always got to say something.

Svava. "Your father, Miss Riis, remains always our man of fashion *par excellence.*"

Riis. Ah, *il a bien dit Son Excellence!* No, then I have something better to tell. You are getting your father knighted.

Svava. Am I?

Riis. Yes, who else? Of course, the government has had some little use for me now and then in connection with various commercial treaties. But this time, as related by marriage to our great man, I become a knight of the Order of St. Olav.

SVAVA. Permit me to congratulate you!

RIIS. You know: when it rains on the parson, it drips on the sexton.

SVAVA. You are most uncommonly modest in your new grandeur.

RIIS. Yes, am I not? And now I am to appear in the modest part of an exhibitor of elegant costumes, or rather designs for costumes—which is still more modest—to be used in the new play at the *Théâtre Français*.

SVAVA. Oh, no, papa! Not just now!

MRS. RIIS. That will have to wait till the afternoon.

RIIS. Really, one might think I was the only lady in the family! Well, as you please—*you* rule the world! But then I have another proposition, in two parts. First: that we sit down!

SVAVA. We are sitting down! [*She and her father take seats.*

RIIS. Then you tell your home-coming papa just how this whole thing happened. All that thing about the "mystery," you know.

SVAVA. Oh, that!—Well, you must excuse me, but it cannot be told.

RIIS. Not in all its charming details! Heaven defend! Nobody would be such a barbarian as to ask for a thing like that during the first honeymoon of the engagement. No, I mean only what was the actual *mobile* back of the whole matter.

SVAVA. Oh, I see. Well, *that* I can tell you, for to know it is merely to become really acquainted with Alf.

RIIS. For instance: how did you come to talk with him at all?

SVAVA. Oh, I think it was about our blessed old kinder- gartens——

RIIS. Oh-h!—You mean *your* blessed old kindergartens?

SVAVA. When there are more than two hundred of us girls——

RIIS. Well, let it go at that! So he contributed?

SVAVA. He contributed, and more than once——

RIIS. Oh-h!

SVAVA. And once we fell to talking about luxury. That it was better to use money in such ways than for mere luxuries.

RIIS. Well, what is to be called "luxury"?

SVAVA. We didn't say anything about that, but I said that I thought luxury immoral.

RIIS. Immo—? Luxury?

SVAVA. Yes, I know that is not your opinion. But it is mine.

RIIS. Your mother's, you mean, and your grandmother's.

SVAVA. Of course; but my own also—if you permit me?

RIIS. Oh, the Lord preserve us!

SVAVA. I told of an incident which mother and you and I witnessed in America—do you remember? At that temperance meeting where we saw ladies who were to support the cause drive up in their carriages—ladies—well, we didn't have any exact figures as to their fortunes, but as they appeared, with their carriages, horses, dresses, jewelry—and especially jewelry—they must have been worth—oh, say——

RIIS. Let us say many, many thousand dollars apiece— that would be true!

SVAVA. It *is* true. And in its way such a thing is as much of an excess as drinking.

RIIS. Oh, well——

SVAVA. Yes, shrug your shoulders! But Alf didn't. He told me what he had seen—in the big cities. It was dreadful!

RIIS. *What* was dreadful?

SVAVA. The chasm yawning between rich and poor—the boundless and reckless display of luxury on one side——

RIIS. Oh, so!—I thought— Well, go on!

SVAVA. He didn't play the indifferent and keep on polishing his nails——

RIIS. I beg pardon!

SVAVA. Please, don't stop!—No, he foretold a great social revolution, and he became quite excited about it—and then it came out how he thought wealth should be used.—It was a complete surprise to me—and much of it was new to me in every way. You should have seen how handsome he looked then!

RIIS. Well—handsome?

SVAVA. Isn't *he* handsome? That's what *I* think, at least! And mamma also——?

MRS. RIIS. [*Without looking up from her periodical*] And mamma also.

RIIS. Mothers always fall in love with their daughters' lovers. But becoming mothers-in-law generally cures them.

SVAVA. Is that *your* experience?

RIIS. That's *my* experience. So Alf Christensen has grown handsome? Well, we'll have to bear with it.

SVAVA. As he was standing before me, he seemed so sure of himself, and so clear in his mind, and so—so chaste—and that is something I demand also.

RIIS. What do you mean by "chaste," my girl?

SVAVA. Just what's in the word.

RIIS. And I am just asking what you put into that word.

SVAVA. The same meaning I should put into it if I were speaking of myself.

RIIS. That is, you put the same meaning into it whether it be applied to a man or a woman?

SVAVA. Of course.

RIIS. And you think that the son of Christensen——

SVAVA. [*Rising*] Papa, now you are offending me!

RIIS. Can it offend you that he is his father's son?

SVAVA. In this respect he is not. It is no longer possible for me to make mistakes in such matters.

MRS. RIIS. I have just been reading about hereditary tendencies—and his heritage need not necessarily have come from his father.

RIIS. Oh, well, as you please! But I am a little fearful on behalf of your superterrestrial theories. I don't think you can get very far with them.

SVAVA. What do you mean—? Mother, what does he mean?

MRS. RIIS. I suppose he means that men are not as you want them to be. And it is no use hoping that they ever will be.

SVAVA. No, you cannot mean that?

RIIS. But why so violent about it? Come and sit down! And besides, how can you know anything about it?

SVAVA. Know?—What *do* you mean?

RIIS. About any individual case——

SVAVA. If the man standing before me, or passing me, is an unclean, repulsive beast—or a man?

RIIS. Etc., etc.! Well, you may be mistaken, my dear Svava.

SVAVA. No, no more than I can be mistaken about you, papa, when you begin to tease me again with those dreadful principles of yours. For in spite of them, you are the finest and cleanest man I know.

MRS. RIIS. [*Putting away the periodical*] Are you going to keep that morning dress on, my dear? Don't you think you had better change before Alf comes?

SVAVA. No, mamma, you can't get me away from this!— For I have had to see more than one of my girl friends nestle close to "the prince of her heart," as the old ballad says, only to wake up in the arms of a beast.—I want none of that. And I am not going to make the same mistake.

MRS. RIIS. There is no reason, dear, to take it so to heart. Alf is an honest young man.

SVAVA. So he is. But I have had to witness one revolting experience after another. And now, only a month ago, the case of Helga. And then I myself—I can tell you all about it now, for now I feel happy and secure—and now I can tell you of the time I once had to go through. There was a long time when I did not dare to trust my own judgment. For I came near letting myself be deceived also.

BOTH PARENTS. [*Rising*] You, Svava?

SVAVA. I was very, very young then. Like most young girls, I was looking for an ideal, and I found it in a brilliant young man—what's the use of naming him? He had—oh, his principles were noble, and his aims of the highest—in this respect he was the complete opposite of papa. It would not be enough to say that I loved him! I worshipped him. But then—oh, I cannot tell you what I discovered, or how I discovered it—but that was the time when all of you feared that I had become——

MRS. RIIS. Consumptive? Is it possible, dear? Was it that time?

SVAVA. Yes, that time— Nobody can endure such deception—nobody can forgive it!

MRS. RIIS. And you told me nothing?

SVAVA. One who has not fallen into the same mistake cannot know what it is to be ashamed of oneself.—Well, it is all over, now. But one thing is sure: that nobody who has had a first experience of such a kind will ever make the same mistake again.

RIIS *has in the meantime left the room.*

MRS. RIIS. Perhaps it was for the best.

SVAVA. I am sure it was— Oh, well, it's over and done with now. But I was not quite done with it until I found Alf.—What became of papa?

MRS. RIIS. Of your father? Why, there he is coming now.

RIIS. [*Comes from the right, with hat on, and busily pulling at one of his gloves*] Listen, children! I simply have to get my trunks out of the custom-house. I am now going down to the station to telegraph about it. You must get yourself ready, too, for the king will soon be coming this way, as you know—and then!—Good-bye, my sweet little girl! [*Kissing her*] You have really made us very, very happy. Otherwise you have some ideas that—oh, well! [*Going toward the door*] Good-bye!

MRS. RIIS. Good-bye!

RIIS. [*Pulling off his glove again*] Did you notice the melody I was playing when you came in? [*Sits down at the piano*] I heard it all over Germany. [*Plays and sings; then breaks off suddenly*] But, good gracious, here is the music, and you can sing and play it yourself. [*Goes out humming.*

SVAVA. Isn't he funny! There is really something innocent about him. Did you notice him last night? He just glittered "with a hundred facets," as they say.

MRS. RIIS. Apparently you couldn't see yourself.

SVAVA. Oh—was I like that?

MRS. RIIS. Your father's daughter—completely.

SVAVA. Yes, mamma, it's no use denying that however great our happiness be, it is made still greater by other people's goodwill. This morning, as I walked along, I was recalling all that had given me pleasure last night, and I found —oh, I can't put it into words. [*She clings closely to her mother.*

MRS. RIIS. My happy little girl!—But now I must look after the house a little.

SVAVA. Do you want me to help you?

MRS. RIIS. By no means.

[*They walk together toward the background.*

SVAVA. Then I'll run through papa's new melody a couple of times—and soon Alf will be here.

MRS. RIIS *goes out to the left.* SVAVA *sits down at the piano.*

FOURTH SCENE

SVAVA. ALF, *from the left.*

ALF. [*Comes in noiselessly and bends down over* SVAVA *so that his face almost touches hers*] What a day that was—yesterday!

SVAVA. [*Rising quickly*] Alf!—But I didn't hear you ring?

ALF. The music—which was beautiful also.

SVAVA. And yesterday—how can I thank you?

[*They move down the stage together.*

ALF. I don't think you have any idea of what a hit you made?

SVAVA. Some, perhaps. But you had better say nothing about it as—it isn't held proper to be aware of it.

ALF. People had to tell me about it, of course, and my father and mother. And to-day everybody is very happy at home.

SVAVA. And here, too!—What is that you are holding in your hand? A letter?

ALF. A letter. The maid who opened the door handed it to me. Some bright wit has figured out that I should probably appear here in the course of the day.

SVAVA. It wasn't very hard to figure out, do you think?

ALF. Not very. It's from Edward Hansen.

SVAVA. Oh, you can take a short cut to his place right through our park.   [*Pointing toward the right.*

ALF. I know. He says it's important, with "important" underlined——

SVAVA. You can take my key—here it is. [*Gives him the key.*

ALF. Thank you, very much!

SVAVA. Oh, it is pure selfishness. I shall have you here again the sooner.

ALF. I'll stay here until dinner-time.

SVAVA. You'll have to stay here longer than that, I tell you, for we have such a lot of things to talk of. About yesterday——

ALF. Yes, I think so, too.

SVAVA. And many other things also.

ALF. I have a very important problem to submit to you.

SVAVA. You have?

ALF. Perhaps you can solve it for me before I return?

SVAVA. Then it cannot be so very knotty.

ALF. Oh, it is. But you have inspirations at times.

SVAVA. Well, what is it?

ALF. Why couldn't we have discovered each other several years ago?

SVAVA. We were not yet ready for each other, of course.

ALF. How can you tell?

SVAVA. From the fact that I myself was not the same then as I am now.

ALF. But there is a natural kinship between those who love each other. I feel it. And it must have existed then as well as now.

SVAVA. Such a natural kinship does not assert itself while you are developing along different lines.

ALF. And so we have been doing—and yet——

SVAVA. And yet we are in love with each other. Because it does not matter how far the roads diverge when, in the end, they meet again.

ALF. In the same way of thinking, you mean?

SVAVA. In such a communion as ours is.

ALF. So very close together?

SVAVA. So very close together!

ALF. But it is just then—when I hold you in my arms as now—that I ask myself over and over again: why have I not done this before?

SVAVA. And I don't give a thought to it—not the least thought. This is the safest place in all the world: that's what I think!

ALF. And without those by-gone years it might not have been so.

SVAVA. What do you mean?

ALF. I mean—oh, I suppose, at bottom, I mean the same as you: that I have not always been what I am now.—But I have to hurry. The letter says I must.

[*They move up the stage.*

SVAVA. It isn't a question of minutes, is it? For there is something I want to tell you first.

ALF. What is it?   [*Stands still.*

SVAVA. When I saw you among all the others, it was at first as if I didn't know you at all. You appeared in a new aspect, as if you had taken on something from the others—in fact, you *were* different.

ALF. Of course! One always is among strangers. When you moved among the other women, it was as if I had never really noticed you before. And, you know, there are certain measures that cannot be taken except when others are present. Only then did I learn whether you were tall or short. Only then did I become aware of a way you have of bending to one side—oh, just a wee bit—as you greet somebody. And your colour—I had seen nothing before——

SVAVA. Now will you stop and give me a chance?

ALF. I will not—oh, here we are again, and I simply *must* leave!   [*They go up the stage again.*

SVAVA. Only a word. You didn't let me finish. When I saw you standing among the other men, it was at first as if I had not recognised you. But just then your glance caught mine, and you nodded to me. I don't know what kind of transformation took place in you or in myself, but I blushed until my face burned. And it was some time before I dared to look at you again.

ALF. And do you know what happened to me? Every time somebody was going to dance with you, I begrudged him the chance of doing so. I didn't seem able to bear it. By heavens, I can't bear that anybody else so much as touches you! [*They embrace*] And yet I have not mentioned the best of all!

SVAVA. And what is that?

ALF. It is this—that when I see you among others—when I catch a glimpse of your arm, for instance—then I say to myself: that arm has been lying around my neck, and there is nobody else in the whole world who can say the same thing. She belongs to me, that girl over there, and to nobody, nobody, nobody else!—That, you see, is the best of all!—But now we are back again in the same spot—it is as if we were bewitched. —Now I *must* go! [*Goes up the stage*] Good-bye! [*Leaves* SVAVA *only to seize hold of her again the next moment*] Why couldn't I have had all this happiness long ago?—Good-bye!

SVAVA. I think I'll go with you.

ALF. Yes, do!

SVAVA. Oh, no, I remember now. I must practise that new song before papa returns. For if I don't do it now, I am sure you will give me no chance later.

[*A ring at the door-bell is heard.*

ALF. Somebody is coming! For heaven's sake, let me get out first!

> *He runs out to the right.* SVAVA *stands looking after him and waving her handkerchief. She is about to return to the piano, when* MARGIT *appears.*

FIFTH SCENE

SVAVA. MARGIT. *Later* HOFF.

MARGIT. There is a gentleman here who wants to——

SVAVA. A gentleman? Don't you know him?

MARGIT. No.

SVAVA. What sort of a gentleman?

MARGIT. Oh, sort of—a little bit——

SVAVA. Suspicious looking?

MARGIT. Oh, no—he's a very nice man.

SVAVA. Tell him that my father is not at home. He has gone down to the station.

MARGIT. I told him so. But it's you, Miss Svava, he wants to speak to.

SVAVA. Ask my mother to come in—oh, well, what's the need of that?—Let him come in.

> [MARGIT *goes out;* HOFF *enters.*

HOFF. It's Miss Riis I am having the honour to—— Yes, I see it is. My name is—Hoff—Karl Hoff. I travel in iron.

SVAVA. But what have I to do with that?

HOFF. Oh, yes—for had I been an ordinary, home-staying fellow, there might have been a lot—that never happened.

SVAVA. What might not have happened?

HOFF. [*Pulls out a large pocket-book and takes from it a tiny letter*] Will you please—would you read this—or perhaps you would rather not?

SVAVA. Well, how can I tell?

HOFF. No, that's so—you must first—if I may?

SVAVA. [*Reading*] "To-night between ten and eleven; that is to say, if the old fool doesn't come home before. Oh, I love you, I love you so much— Put a light in the hall window."

HOFF. "The old fool"—that's me.

SVAVA. But I don't see——

HOFF. Here's another.

SVAVA. "I am suffering from bad conscience. Your cough scares me. And now when you are expecting—" But what in the world have I to do with all this?

HOFF. [*After some hesitation*] Well, what do you think?

SVAVA. Is there anybody who needs my help?

HOFF. No, poor thing, she needs no more helping. She's dead.

SVAVA. Dead? She was your wife?

HOFF. That's it. She was my wife.—I found these and some other things in—in a box. The papers were furthest down—there's more of them—and then some cotton on top of them. Then there were ear-rings and such things which she had got from her mother. And then—these bracelets. I guess they cost too much to come from her mother.

SVAVA. She must have died suddenly then, as she hadn't time——

HOFF. Oh, I don't know. Consumptives never think they're going to die.—She was such a weak, delicate thing.— Do you mind if I sit down?

SVAVA. Not at all! Are there any children?

HOFF. [*After some hesitation*] I don't think so.

SVAVA. You don't think—? The reason I ask was that I thought our kindergarten society— Frankly, this is painful to me!

HOFF. I thought it would be—yes, I thought it would—and really I don't know if— Oh, *you* can't understand all this, can you?

SVAVA. No, I cannot.

HOFF. No, of course, you can't— I have heard so many fine things said of you these last years—and my wife used to speak that way of you, too.

SVAVA. Did she know me?

HOFF. Maren Tang—she that was lady companion to——

SVAVA. ——to Mrs. Christensen, who is to be my mother-in-law? Oh, it was she? That very quiet, refined woman— Don't you think you are mistaken? A couple of notes without any name—without a date even? Don't you——?

HOFF. Could you recognise the handwriting?

SVAVA. I?—No.—And it looked as if it had been disguised.

HOFF. Well—but not so very much.

SVAVA. But you must have had some definite purpose in calling on me?

HOFF. So I had.—But I guess I won't bother about it. You don't understand this kind of thing, I can see.—Maybe you just think me a little off?—And maybe we might let it go at that?

SVAVA. But there was *something* you wanted?

HOFF. Yes, that's so. You see, these kindergartens——

SVAVA. So it was the kindergartens after all?

HOFF. No, that wasn't it. But on account of them I kind of thought a lot of you, you see. And if you don't mind my saying it: young ladies of the better class who do something useful—well, I had never heard of it before. Never before.— I am nothing but a poor fellow who's failed in his own business and now has to travel for others—not much good for anything, I dare say—and maybe I deserved what I got.— But just the same I wanted to see *you* kept out of it. I kind

of thought it was my duty—nothing less than my duty—
But now, when I see you sitting like that before me—then it
makes me unhappy all through.   And so I don't want to say
anything to you at all. [*Rising*] Nothing at all!

SVAVA. This is something I cannot understand.

HOFF. Now, don't you pay any attention to me at all.
All I ask you is to excuse me—excuse me very much!—No,
please don't give yourself any trouble!   Not at all!   It's just
as if I hadn't been here.   That's all.

> *He goes toward the door, where he meets* ALF; *seeing that*
> SVAVA *is watching them, he hurries out.*

SIXTH SCENE

SVAVA.   ALF.   *Later* RIIS.

SVAVA. [*As she watches the two men meeting, she gives vent to
a subdued cry.   Then she goes quickly toward* ALF. *But when
she stands face to face with him, she seems to be seized with terror.
He approaches her in order to support her, but she cries out*]
Don't touch me! [*She tries to reach the door on the left, but
seems for a moment unable to find it.   Then she hurries out and
is heard locking the door from within.   Shortly afterward the
sound of violent crying is heard, but rendered faint by distance.
It lasts only a moment.   Then somebody on the outside is heard
singing the melody already familiar to the audience, and a few
moments later* RIIS *appears on the stage*]

Curtain.

ACT II

The same room as in the previous act.

FIRST SCENE

SVAVA. MRS. RIIS.

SVAVA is reclining on the right-hand sofa so that she rests on one arm and has her face turned toward the park. MRS. RIIS is sitting beside the sofa, facing her daughter.

MRS. RIIS. These sudden decisions, Svava, are in reality no decisions at all. For there is always so much that comes after.—Take time to think! I believe him to be a pretty fine man. Give him time to show it. Don't break off at once.

SVAVA. Why are you constantly telling me this?

MRS. RIIS. But, dear girl, I have really had no chance to tell you anything at all until now.

SVAVA. But all your remarks have been set to the same tune.

MRS. RIIS. And what tune would you prefer?

SVAVA. The old one—your own—which is quite different.

MRS. RIIS. It is one thing to teach one's child how to choose among life's offerings——

SVAVA. And another to stick to one's own teachings?

MRS. RIIS. Another thing it is to live. Then it is sometimes necessary to make allowances, especially when two are to live together.

SVAVA. In minor matters this is all right.

MRS. RIIS. Only in minor matters——?

SVAVA. Yes, in regard to peculiarities and such things that

44

are mere accidentals. But not when it is a question of essential development.

Mrs. Riis. Then, too.

Svava. Then, too? But we marry only to develop ourselves. Why should we otherwise marry at all?

Mrs. Riis. You'll find out.

Svava. No, I won't. For I am not going to marry.

Mrs. Riis. You should have said that before. Now it is too late.

Svava. [*Half rising from the sofa*] Too late? Had I been married twenty years, I should be doing exactly the same thing.
[*Lies down again.*

Mrs. Riis. Oh, Lord preserve us!—You don't know—no, you don't know at all into what kind of net you have stumbled. But you'll discover it the moment you try in earnest to tear yourself loose.—Or do you really want your father to throw away everything we have built up here? Do you want us to start all over again in a strange country? For he has repeatedly declared during the last few days, that the disgrace of a breach is something which he cannot face. He means to leave, and if he does, I shall have to go with him.— Yes, now you are twisting and turning in the net! And think of the others! It is a little dangerous to be made so much of as you were at the engagement party. It is as if you had been lifted up on a platform supported by all the others. Take care lest they push you down again! And you may be sure they will, if you violate their ideas of propriety.

Svava. And is this their idea of propriety?

Mrs. Riis. Not exactly. But that no scandal be caused is inevitably one of those ideas, and perhaps the first of all.— Nobody takes kindly to a disgraceful exposure. Particularly those that are most powerful. And least of all do people like to see their children disgraced.

SVAVA. [*Half rising*] But, good Lord, am *I* disgracing *him* ?

MRS. RIIS. No, I suppose he is doing it himself——

SVAVA. Well!   [*Drops back again.*

MRS. RIIS. But you will never make them see it that way.
—No, you won't.—As long as only the family and a few close
friends are whispering about what has happened, they don't
regard it as any disgrace at all. For the same thing is happen-
ing in too many other places. It is only when it becomes
known to all the world that they look upon it as a disgrace.
And if there should be a breach, and the cause of it become
known—that the eldest son of the Christensens had been
ignominiously jilted on account of his past—then they would
regard this as the worst scandal that could ever befall them.—
And we should have to suffer for it. We, and every one de-
pendent on us. And you know, they are not a few. You
have taken them under your care, especially the children.
But then you would have to let all those go that you have
helped. For you would have to follow us. And I am sure
that your father is in earnest about leaving.

SVAVA. O-oh!

MRS. RIIS. I wish I could tell you why I am so sure of it.
But I cannot—not just now, at least— No, you mustn't ask
me to do so— There is your father now. Take time to
think, Svava. No breach! No scandal!

SECOND SCENE

SVAVA. MRS. RIIS. RIIS comes from the outside with
an open letter in his hand.

RIIS. Oh, lying down a little, are you? [*Goes into his room
to deposit hat and stick, and then returns*] Nothing serious, I
hope?

MRS. RIIS. No, but——

RIIS. Well, here is a letter from the Christensens now. As you don't want to see Alf, or even receive letters from him, you have to be prepared for the interference of his family. There's an end to everything, of course. [*Reads*] "My wife, my son and I will have the honour of calling on you between eleven and twelve."—It's a wonder that this hasn't happened long before. They have shown a great deal of patience, I think.

MRS. RIIS. We, on our side, haven't got any further than we were before.

RIIS. But what are you thinking of, Svava? Can't you see where *this* kind of thing must lead to? You have a heart in you, I know, and I am sure you don't want to ruin all of us? Really, it seems to me, Svava, that you have shown all the firmness that could possibly be needful in this case. Their self-assurance has been shaken down to its very roots —you can depend on it. What more do you want? Or do you actually want to push the matter still farther? Well, name your conditions. In all likelihood they will be accepted.

SVAVA. Oh, faugh!

RIIS. [*In despair*] Well, it just won't do to take it that way!

MRS. RIIS. No, it won't, Svava! You should rather try to meet them half-way.

RIIS. And, really, you should deign to consider what you are throwing away. One of the richest families in the country, and also one of the most honourable, I dare say. I have never heard of any indiscretions on their part. Yes, that's what I say. No indiscretions, I say. There may have been a lapse—or more than one—but then—good Lord!

SVAVA. Yes, bring Him in, too!

RIIS. Yes, that's just what I mean to do. For the matter

is serious enough. Even if there has been a lapse of some kind,
I say, the poor young fellow has been punished hard enough
for it. And, after all, we have to be a little reasonable, and
forgive. We *have* to forgive. And more than that. We
have to help those that err—we have to raise up those that
fall—we have to set them on the right path— Yes, set them
on the right path! And that's a thing *you* can do so beauti-
fully. You are just made for it.—As you probably know,
my dear, it doesn't happen very often that I talk morality or
that sort of thing. Frankly speaking, it isn't becoming to
me, and I feel it perfectly. But on this occasion I simply
cannot refrain.—Begin by forgiving, my child—that's what
you should begin with! And besides, can you imagine a
continued life together without some—without some—well,
without *that?*

SVAVA. But there is no question here about any continued
life together—or about forgiving either. Because I don't
want to have anything more to do with him.

RIIS. But this passes all limits!—Because he has dared to
love somebody else before you——?

SVAVA. Somebody?

RIIS. Yes, no more than that, so far as I am aware of.—
No, not a thing more! And it beats the deuce, the way people
run around with slander and gossip. But what I say is this:
because he dared to look at somebody else before he looked
at you, or before he ever *thought* of you, that's no reason why
he should be eternally condemned. How many could then
get married, I might venture to ask. Everybody declares
him to be such a fine and honest young fellow that the proud-
est girl in the world could trust him with her faith—yes, and
that's just what you said yourself a while ago! Don't deny
it! But now he is all of a sudden to be utterly spurned because *you* don't happen to be the first woman he met.—

There should be some limit to pride as well as to everything else. And I, for my part, have never heard of anything more unreasonable.

MRS. RIIS. That's not the men's way.

RIIS. And how about the girls? What is their way? They don't care whether the man to whom they become engaged has been married before—ah, there I happened to use the word married. You may simply regard him as having been married before. And why not? That's what other girls do. Well, it's no use denying it! For I know that you know it! You have danced at more than one ball, haven't you? And what men are most sought after on such occasions? Exactly those—those whose names are smilingly connected with that of Don Juan. They take the wind out of the sails of everybody else. You have seen it yourself a hundred times.—And does it happen only at balls? Don't such men marry? As a rule *they* make the best marriages of all.

MRS. RIIS. That's true.

RIIS. Of course, it is true. And as a rule they become pretty good husbands at that.

MRS. RIIS. Hm-m?

RIIS. Oh, yes, indeed, they do!—Well, good gracious, there are exceptions! But the truth of the matter is, that marriage has an ennobling influence. And just here we meet with woman's highest mission. The very highest of all her missions!

SVAVA. [*Who has risen*] Oh, if need be, I can listen to that kind of thing from you. For I have expected nothing better.

RIIS. Thanks very much!

SVAVA. [*Coming down the stage*] One might think that marriage was a sort of higher ablutionary institution for men——

RIIS. Ha, ha!

SVAVA. And that men had a right to throw themselves into it just when they wanted—and in any manner suiting them.

RIIS. Oh, no——

SVAVA. Oh, yes—and it is flattering—so very flattering to me, your own daughter, that you hold me particularly fitted for that kind of higher laundry work.   Nevertheless I shall have nothing to do with it.

RIIS. But this beats——

SVAVA. Now you listen to me a little!   I don't think I have been talking too much these days.

RIIS. No, we haven't been able to get a word out of you.

SVAVA. You, papa—you carry around a lot of principles for exhibition purposes.

RIIS. For what?

SVAVA. By which I don't mean to say that they are not yours.   But you are so good, so honest, so refined in everything you do, that I don't care a rap about your principles. But I do care about mother's.   For she has formed my own. And when I want to apply them, she runs away.

MRS. RIIS *and* RIIS. But, Svava——!

SVAVA. It is mother I am angry with—it is her I cannot bear with.

RIIS. Really, Svava!

SVAVA. For if there be any one thing about which mother and I have been especially agreed, it is the unseemly way in which men prepare themselves for marriage—and about the marriages which are the outcome of it.   We have been following up this matter for many years, mother and I.   And both of us have become convinced that it is *before* marriage most marriages are spoiled.—And then, when mother began to change her tone a while ago——

MRS. RIIS. No, you can't say I have done that.   For I believe Alf is honest——

SVAVA. When mother began to change her tone—well, I could not have been more surprised if somebody had come and told me that he had met mother on the street while she was sitting here talking with me.

MRS. RIIS. But all I ask is that you take time. I don't oppose you.

SVAVA. No, let me speak now.—Just one instance! Once, when I was about half-grown, I came running in here from the park. We had recently bought the place, and I was very happy about it. And then I found mother standing here, leaning up against the door and crying. It was a beautiful summer evening. "Why are you crying, mamma?" I asked. For a long while she pretended not to see me. Then I went closer to her and asked again: "Why are you crying, mamma?" But I never touched her. She turned away from me and walked back and forth several times. Then she came up to me. "Child," she said, and drew me close to herself. "Never give up anything of what you think good and right—not for any price! It's the most cowardly thing you can do, and you'll regret it terribly. For you will have to give up more and more and more." I don't know what she had in mind: I have never asked her. But the summer evening, and mother crying, and her words—the force of those words—it would be impossible to exaggerate what the memory of it all has been to me. *I* cannot give up anything. Don't ask it of me!—Everything that made marriage beautiful to me is gone. My faith, my trust—gone! No, no! This cannot be the way in which it should begin. And it is sinful of you to try to persuade me. To reach it through such disappointment—such humiliation? No, then I'll rather remain un-married—even if it be in a strange country. I can find some-thing to fill up my life with, I am sure. It is only for the moment I feel lost. And anything is better than to fill up one's life with impurity. If you don't reject such things at once, you become guilty of them yourself. Perhaps there are those who can bear such things. Not I. No, I cannot!— You think it is pride. Because I am angry. But if you knew what he and I had agreed and planned—then you might understand! And if you knew what I have thought of him, how high up I had placed him—well, then you might also understand how unhappy I am now! How boundless my loss is!—Who's crying? Mother!— [SVAVA *runs across the stage, kneels down beside her mother and puts her head in her lap; long silence;* RIIS *goes out to the right*] Why cannot we three stick together? If we do, what have we to fear? What could happen? Papa, what could happen?—Where is papa? [*Catches sight of* DR. NORDAN *outside*] Uncle Nordan! Well, I never expected! [*She runs up the stage to meet him, throws herself into his arms and bursts into tears*]

THIRD SCENE

SVAVA. MRS. RIIS. DR. NORDAN. *Later* RIIS.

NORDAN. Oh, you little goose! You dear, silly little goose!

SVAVA. Oh, you've got to talk to me now!

NORDAN. Well, why do you think I am here?

SVAVA. And I who thought you were up in the mountains and couldn't be reached!

NORDAN. Well, where do you think I was? But telegram after telegram, as far as they could reach—and then messenger after messenger—and then, last of all—but I suppose, I dare not even mention his name now?

RIIS. [*Who has reappeared from the right*] At last! The way we have been waiting for you!

MRS. RIIS. [*Who finally has risen and come forward*] Thank you for coming, dear doctor!

NORDAN. [*Looking at* MRS. RIIS] There must be stormy days here.

MRS. RIIS. *You* don't need to be told anything.

NORDAN. Well, off with you now, both of you! Let Noodlekin and me have it out between ourselves.

MRS. RIIS *goes out to the left, accompanied by* SVAVA.

RIIS. All I want to say is that in a little while——

NORDAN. ——comes the whole Christensen host. I know! Go now!

RIIS. [*Whispering*] Nordan!

NORDAN. Yes, yes—oh, yes—no, of course not! [*Drawing away from* RIIS] Don't you think I know all that? Get out of here!

As RIIS *goes out to the right,* SVAVA *returns from the left.*

SVAVA. Dear Uncle Nordan—at last I shall have somebody who agrees with me!

NORDAN. Oh, that's what you expect?

SVAVA. Oh, uncle, what days these have been!

NORDAN. And nights, I suppose?—Although you don't look so very bad after all.

SVAVA. I have slept the last couple of nights.

NORDAN. Oh, you have! Then I think I see how the matter stands.—You are a tough one, you are!

SVAVA. Don't begin now to say a lot of things you don't mean, uncle!

NORDAN. That I don't mean?

SVAVA. For that's what you always do. And we haven't time for it now. I am on burning coals.

NORDAN. Well, what haven't you gone and stirred up?

SVAVA. There you begin now!

NORDAN. Begin? Who the deuce has made you believe

that I say anything but what I mean? Come now and let's sit down! [*He places a chair in the middle of the floor.*

SVAVA. [*Putting her chair near his but at a right angle to it*] All right!

NORDAN. I understand that since I saw you last, you have issued a brand-new commandment in regard to love. My congratulations!

SVAVA. Have I?

NORDAN. A supernatural, Svava-istic one. Probably devised from the science of spherical harmonics. "There is but one love, and it has but one object." *Dixi!*

SVAVA. Have *I* said that?

NORDAN. Are you not spurning a young man because he has dared to love before he saw you?

SVAVA. So *you* are also regarding it in that manner?

NORDAN. In *that* manner? As if among rational people there were any other? A splendid young fellow actually worships you. One of our best families fling their double doors wide open for you as if you were a princess. And then you retort: "You haven't been waiting for me ever since you were a little boy—*avaunt!*"

SVAVA. [*Rising abruptly*] Oh, you too, you too! And the same text! The same stupid old text!

NORDAN. I may as well tell you this much at once: if you don't take into consideration what can be said against you, then you are a fool. It's no use whatever for you to rush away from me and begin prancing up and down. For then I'll begin to prance also. Come here and sit down. Or perhaps you don't *dare* to study the question more closely?

SVAVA. Oh, yes, I dare! [*She sits down beside him again.*

NORDAN. For suppose now that the question happens to be an extremely unsettled one, which is being discussed by serious men and women all over the world?

SVAVA. But it concerns me alone. And to me it isn't unsettled at all.

NORDAN. You misunderstand me, child! In the last instance, you have to decide on your own case—you, and nobody else. Of course! But when what you are to decide on is not quite as clear as you may think; when, at this very moment, it is occupying the minds of thousands and thousands—is it not your duty then to show some regard for prevailing conditions, and for what is generally said and thought about them? Is it not unconscionable, without some such regard, to judge the individual case?

SVAVA. I see! And I think that what you demand of me I have already done. Ask my mother.

NORDAN. Oh, yes, you and your mother have talked and read a whole lot about marriage, and woman's emancipation, and the abolition of special privileges for special classes—and now all privileges of sex are also to be abolished. But what about the particular question at issue?

SVAVA. What is it you think I have overlooked?

NORDAN. This! Have you the right to be as exacting toward man as toward woman? What do you say?

SVAVA. Yes, of course!

NORDAN. Is it really so much a matter of course? Suppose you were to make some inquiries. Of a hundred people you asked, ninety would answer "no"—*even among the women themselves!*

SVAVA. I don't know—it's beginning to change.

NORDAN. Very well. But knowledge is needed after all to settle the question.

SVAVA. Do you really mean what you are saying?

NORDAN. Never mind! And for that matter, I always mean what I say.—A woman can marry at sixteen. A man has to wait until he is twenty-five or thirty.—That makes a difference!

SVAVA. There is a difference! For we have many, many, many more unmarried women than men. And these women are showing themselves capable of self-control—while the men find it easier to make a law out of their lack of self-control.

NORDAN. That kind of talk shows nothing but ignorance. The human creature is a polygamous animal, just like many other ones, and this theory is strongly supported by the fact that we have so many more women than men. This is something you have never heard before, I guess?

SVAVA. Yes, doctor, I have!

NORDAN. Don't laugh at science! What the deuce are we to believe in otherwise?

SVAVA. If you would only let the men have as much trouble with their children as the women? Why don't you let them, uncle? Then I think we would soon have a new set of principles. Oh, just let them, uncle!

NORDAN. They haven't the time. They must run the world.

SVAVA. Yes, they have chosen their own part!—But tell me, *Doctor* Nordan: is it not cowardly not to live in accordance with one's own teachings? [*She kneels down beside him.*

NORDAN. Yes, of course, it's cowardly!

SVAVA. Why, then, don't you live in accordance with yours?

NORDAN. I? Why, I have always been a monster! Don't you know that, dear?

SVAVA. Dearest Uncle Nordan—you have such long white locks—why do you let your hair grow that way?

NORDAN. Oh—there are reasons!

SVAVA. And what reasons?

NORDAN. Don't let us talk of that now.

SVAVA. But you have already told me.

NORDAN. Have I?

SVAVA. I wanted to touch your hair once, and you wouldn't let me.   And then you said: "Do you know why I won't let you do it?"—"No," said I.—"Because nobody else has done so for thirty-four years."—"Who was the last one that touched it?" I asked.—"It was a little girl whom you resemble," you answered.

NORDAN. No, did I really tell you that?

SVAVA. "And she was a younger sister of your grandmother," you said to me.

NORDAN. So she was.   Yes, yes, so she was.   And you resemble her, child.

SVAVA. And then you told me that once—the year you entered the university—she was standing beside you and held as much as she could of your hair in one of her hands.   And then she said: "You must never wear your hair shorter than it is now."—She went her way, and you went yours.   And a little while afterward you wrote and asked her if you two hadn't better stick together for life.   And she answered, yes.   But a month later she died.

NORDAN. Did she die?

SVAVA. And ever since, this funny Uncle Nordan has considered himself married to her. [NORDAN *nods*] And the very night when you told me this—and when I lay awake so long, thinking it over and over—then I made up my mind that I should early choose one in whom I could place my whole trust— And I chose badly.

NORDAN. No, did you, Svava?

SVAVA. Don't ask me about it now!—But then I chose again, and felt secure.   For never did a pair of eyes look more faithfully into another.—And the way we had everything in common!   Day after day, each one bringing some new discovery, each one seeming too short. Oh, I dare not think of it now!—It is a sin to deceive in that way: not with words, to be sure, but by permitting us to dream and to surrender ourselves. No, not with words. And yet with words, too. For don't they listen to our words, and say nothing, and so make them their own? They take pleasure in our innocence as in a piece of unspoiled nature—and just by so doing, they deceive us. For the result of it is a certain intimacy, a certain mutual banter, that can only have one basis— that is, as we see it. And then it turns out to be ambiguous after all.—I don't understand how anybody can act like that toward one whom he loves? For he did love me!

NORDAN. And he does now!

SVAVA. [*Rising*] But not as I loved him! *I* had not been giving myself away by piecemeal during the passing years. My thoughts of love, and of being loved, were too high for that. But for that very reason my desire was strong.—Oh, to you I dare say so. And when it was free, it nearly swept me off my feet. But I felt so absolutely safe with him, and so I let him see it, and I took pleasure in his seeing it.—It is this that hurts me now. For he was not worthy of it. He said to me: I cannot bear that anybody else touches you. He said to me: when I catch a glimpse of your arm, then I remember that it has been lying around my neck, and that nobody, nobody else can say the same.—And I felt happy and proud at hearing him say it: for it was true. A hundred times I had told myself that somebody would say just that to me some time. But what I had not thought was that the man speaking thus to me would himself—oh, abominable! Then it gets a meaning that makes me hate him! Yes, the mere thought that he has had his arms about me, that he has touched me—it sets me trembling to my innermost soul! —I lay down no rules for others. But the rule for myself springs from my own self. My whole nature, from beginning to end, determines it. Let *me* alone!

NORDAN. This is more serious and goes deeper than I had any idea of. Nobody else looks at the matter in such a way, and Alf least of all. He merely feels hurt—hurt and insulted because you don't trust him.

SVAVA. I know it.

NORDAN. Well, don't be so brusque about it. For it is just the way most people would feel about it.

SVAVA. Hm-m?

NORDAN. Most of them would think: other girls forgive that sort of thing—just because they love.

SVAVA. And some would answer: had she *not* loved, she might also have forgiven.

NORDAN. And yet, Svava? And yet——?

SVAVA. But, uncle, can't you understand! And I fear I cannot explain it to you. For to do so, I should be able to explain what it is we put into a man's appearance, nature, walk, when we love him—into his voice, into his smile. And it is just this that is gone. The meaning of it all is gone.

NORDAN. For a while, yes—until you have had time to breathe——

SVAVA. No, no, no! Do you recall a song I have often been singing to you—about the image of the loved one? How it always appears with a burst of joy, as if bathed in joy? Do you recall it?

NORDAN. Yes.

SVAVA. Well then—*that* is just what it doesn't do any longer! It does appear, of course; but only pain comes with it.— Always!—And a thing like that should be forgiven? Because other girls have forgiven? But did they then never love, those other girls? Can you tell me that? For what I have loved is gone. And I don't intend to sit down and try to dream it back again. I shall find something else to occupy myself with.

NORDAN. Well, you are in a bitter mood now. Your ideal has been thoroughly smashed. And, of course, it's of no use to talk as long as the pain of it lasts. And for that reason—only one thing—one single little thing—but that one thing you must promise me!

SVAVA. If I can.

NORDAN. You can. There are many things to be considered here. Ask for time to think it over.

SVAVA. Oh—mother has written to you.

NORDAN. Well, what of it? Your mother knows what is at stake here.

SVAVA. At stake? You talk so mysteriously as if we were not safe? Are we not? My father speaks of leaving the country. Why?

NORDAN. I suppose he thinks himself compelled to do so.

SVAVA. My father? For economical reasons?

NORDAN. Not at all! No, but you will have to face a lot of hostile gossip. For there is a challenge in what you do.

SVAVA. Oh, we are not afraid of criticism!—Of course, my father has very peculiar principles, as you know. But as far as his life is concerned—? I hope nobody has any doubt on that score?

NORDAN. Now listen, girl; nobody can prevent people from making up things. Be careful!

SVAVA. What *do* you mean?

NORDAN. I mean that you ought to take a walk in the park and pull yourself together a little before the Christensens are at the door. Try to calm yourself down, and then come in and ask for a little more time. That's all! They will grant what you ask—because they are forced to. Nothing has happened, and every road remains open. Do that now!

SVAVA. I *have* thought. And you will never bring me around.

NORDAN. All right—then what remains is nothing but a formality?

SVAVA. Hm-m? There is something else behind what you say.

NORDAN. My, but you are wilful! Can't you do this—for your mother's sake, let us say? Your *mother* is a very good woman.

SVAVA. What are they to think when I come in and say: "Please give me a little more time!"—Oh, no, I cannot!

NORDAN. Well, what would you say?

SVAVA. Nothing at all, if I could choose. But if I must——

NORDAN. Of course, you must!

SVAVA. Then I'll go out and think it over. [*As she goes toward the door*] But it won't be what you want.

NORDAN. [*Who remains standing on the same spot as before*] But it must be just that!

SVAVA. [*Stopping at the door*] You said: Your mother is a very good woman—that's what you said. It seemed as if you were putting stress on *mother?*

NORDAN. Well?

SVAVA. And my father?

NORDAN. A good woman—your father?

SVAVA. Why do you try to evade it with a jest?

NORDAN. Oh, hang it, because it is serious, of course!

SVAVA. Is my father not to be trusted——?

NORDAN. Sh!

SVAVA. My father?—Could it be possible that—? Is that what people are saying? [*When* DR. NORDAN *remains silent and motionless*] It's a shame! Impossible! Impossible, I say! [*She goes out quickly.*

FOURTH SCENE

NORDAN.   RIIS *comes from the right.*

RIIS. What is the matter with Svava?

NORDAN. [*Walking back and forth*] There was nothing else to do.

RIIS. [*Following him*] Nothing else to do? But what?

NORDAN. No, I'll be darned if there was anything else to do!

RIIS. Is that so? But what was it?

NORDAN. What did you say?

RIIS. No, *you* said——

NORDAN. What did *I* say?

RIIS. You said that there was nothing else to do—— And you quite scared me.

NORDAN. Did I? Well, you didn't hear right.

[*Goes away from him.*

RIIS. Didn't I? Why, you even said you would be darned!

NORDAN. I didn't do anything of the kind.

RIIS. Well, then you didn't.—But what happened with Svava? Can't you tell me?

NORDAN. What happened with Svava?

RIIS. Why are you so preoccupied? Did things go wrong?

NORDAN. Preoccupied? Why should I be?

RIIS. Well, you know best.   But I was asking about Svava. What happened with Svava? It seems to me I have a right to know!

NORDAN. You, Riis?

RIIS. Yes. [*As* NORDAN *puts his arm through his*] What is it now?

NORDAN. Did you see Svava?

RIIS. As she rushed out into the park? Yes.—My dear fellow, what was it?

NORDAN. It was the Greek tragedy.

RIIS. The Gr——?

NORDAN. Just the name. Just the name. You know what it means, don't you?

RIIS. Something sad?

NORDAN. Not at all! Something very funny! It came to Greece with the cult of Dionysos. And in his train there was a goat——

RIIS. [*Pulling his arm away*] A—? But what——?

NORDAN. Yes, you may well be surprised. For the goat sang.

RIIS. He—sang?

NORDAN. Yes, and he is singing still, don't you know—and painting—oh! His pictures appear in every exhibition. And he works in bronze and marble. Splendidly! And what a courtier he is! He designs the costumes and decides what society——

RIIS. Have you gone clear out of your head?

NORDAN. Why so?

RIIS. I am merely waiting for all that damned nonsense to blow over. Of course, we are accustomed to almost anything when you are in this mood, but to-night I cannot understand a blessed word of what you are saying.

NORDAN. Oh, my dear fellow, is that so?

RIIS. Can't you tell me what my daughter said? It's perfectly ridiculous that I can't find out! Now, be brief and plain: what did she say?

NORDAN. You want to know that?

RIIS. And he asks me that·

NORDAN. She said: it is a pity about all the innocent little girls that, generation after generation, come tripping along. That's what she said.

RIIS. Tripping where?

NORDAN. That's just it: where? And she said: they are brought up in pious ignorance, and finally those trustful ones are swathed in a long, white veil, in order that they may not see where they are going.

RIIS. But this is mythology again. Why can't you——

NORDAN. Listen! It's your daughter speaking— *But I will not*, she said. I will walk securely into holy matrimony and sit beside the hearth of my native land and rear children before the sight of my husband. But he must be chaste as I am, or he will defile my child's head when he kisses it, and to me he will bring dishonour.—Now, that's what she said, and when she said it, she looked so beautiful!

[*A door-bell is heard ringing.*

RIIS. Now, there they are! There they are! How in the world is this going to end? We are immersed in the most unreasonable theories! We are buzzing about in the midst of a gigantic mythology! [*Rushes toward the door.*

FIFTH SCENE

DR. NORDAN. RIIS. MR. *and* MRS. CHRISTENSEN. MRS. RIIS. MARGIT. *Later* ALF.

RIIS. [*Meeting the new-comers and speaking while they are still outside*] Welcome! I wish you welcome of all my heart! —But where is your son?

CHRISTENSEN. [*Still outside*] We couldn't make him come.

RIIS. I am very sorry. Although, of course, I understand.

CHRISTENSEN. [*Appearing in the doorway*] Every time I

come here, I have to admire your splendid place over again, my dear Riis.

MRS. CHRISTENSEN. Oh, this old park! I wish that in due time— Ah, doctor—how is everything going?

NORDAN. So-o-o——

RIIS. [*To* MARGIT, *who has followed the guests in*] Please tell Mrs. Riis—will you? And—oh, there she is! [MRS. RIIS *enters through the door on the left*] And Miss Svava.

NORDAN. She is out in the park—over to the right!

[MARGIT *leaves.*

RIIS. No, the other way!—That's it!—Walk straight ahead till you find her!

MRS. CHRISTENSEN. [*Simultaneously to* MRS. RIIS *as both come down the stage*] Oh, my dear, I have thought of *you* so much these days! Such an annoying story!

MRS. RIIS. May I ask if you knew anything about it before?

MRS. CHRISTENSEN. What hasn't a mother—and a wife—to know these days, dear? As you may recall, she was in my house. Come here a moment!

> *She relates something in whispers, gradually raising her voice a little, so that toward the end such words can be heard as "discovery" and "turned out."*

RIIS. [*Offering chairs to the ladies*] If you please!—Oh, beg your pardon, I didn't see— [*Rushes over to* CHRISTENSEN] Excuse me, but are you really comfortable there, tell me?

CHRISTENSEN. Thanks, it's as bad here as anywhere else. For it's mainly this sitting down and getting up again that gives me trouble. [*After looking around*] I have been to see him.

RIIS. Whom—Hoff?

CHRISTENSEN. Decent chap. Stupid.

RIIS. Well, if he only keeps his mouth shut——

CHRISTENSEN. He will.

RIIS. Thank heaven! Then it's all between ourselves.—I suppose it cost something?

CHRISTENSEN. Not a cent!

RIIS. Why, you got out of that cheap.

CHRISTENSEN. Yes, didn't I?—However, it has cost me plenty before—but *he* knows nothing of that.

RIIS. Oh? When he failed?

CHRISTENSEN. No, when he married.

RIIS. Oh, I see!

CHRISTENSEN. And I thought that ended the story. What kind of whispering game are the ladies playing?

MRS. CHRISTENSEN. [*Coming toward the centre of the stage;* RIIS *arranges chairs for her and for his wife*] I was telling about this matter with Miss Tang. One might almost say she had risen out of her grave.

CHRISTENSEN. Pardon me, but—isn't your daughter at home?

RIIS. We have sent for her.

MRS. CHRISTENSEN. I hope she, too, has learned a thing or two these days, poor thing! She has been suffering from a fault that often belongs to very clever people—I mean self-righteousness.

RIIS. Exactly! Quite right! Call it arrogance!

MRS. CHRISTENSEN. No, I wouldn't call it that. But pride, perhaps.

MRS. RIIS. What makes you think so?

MRS. CHRISTENSEN. Several talks I have had with her. Once I spoke of the husband as our lord and master. In these days of new-fangled ideas it is just as well to impress such things on our young girls.

CHRISTENSEN. Yes, the Lord knows!

MRS. CHRISTENSEN. And when I reminded her of what Paul said, she replied: "Yes, those are the bars behind which we women still are imprisoned." Then I knew that something was bound to happen sooner or later. Pride always goes before a fall.

CHRISTENSEN. No, dear—no. That line of reasoning don't hold. No, really!

MRS. CHRISTENSEN. Oh, is that so?

CHRISTENSEN. No! For first of all, it was not Miss Riis that fell, but your own darling son. Secondly, he didn't fall on account of Miss Riis's pride—in fact, I think he fell several years before Miss Riis gave vent to her pride. So that when you knew that his fall would result from Miss Riis's pride, then you knew something that you didn't know at all.

MRS. CHRISTENSEN. Yes, you scoff!

CHRISTENSEN. Oh, I have to attend a committee meeting at one sharp. May I ask what has become of your daughter?

RIIS. Yes, I am also beginning to——

NORDAN. [*Who has kept in the background, sometimes in the room and sometimes outside, says now to* MARGIT, *who is just passing by the door from right to left*] Didn't you find her until now?

MARGIT. Yes, I have been down once before with Miss Svava's hat and parasol.

NORDAN. Is she going out?

MARGIT. I don't know.   [*Goes.*

CHRISTENSEN. Well, well!

RIIS. What's the meaning of this?

[*Is about to leave the room.*

NORDAN. No, no! Not you!

MRS. RIIS. [*Has risen and goes toward the door*] I think I had better——

RIIS. Yes, you go!

NORDAN. No, *I* will go! For I fear I have been the cause—[*Going*] I promise to bring her back.

CHRISTENSEN. Well, well!

MRS. CHRISTENSEN. [*Rising*] I fear, my dear, that our visit is inconveniencing the young lady?

RIIS. You must have forbearance with her! It comes from all these romantic ideas, I tell you; from all this reading which her mother has not held properly in check.

MRS. RIIS. I? What is it you are saying?

RIIS. I am saying that this is an important moment. And such moments seem to bring clearness—just as if—yes, they do!

CHRISTENSEN. Your husband, Mrs. Riis, seems to have had the same revelation which came to our minister recently —that is, to my wife's minister. It was just after dinner—a very good dinner, too—and that's a time when brilliant ideas are likely to come. We were talking about how much more woman has to learn now than she had in the past. It didn't matter much, said somebody, for she forgot all about it as soon as she was married. And then the minister cried out joyfully: "Yes, my wife has already forgotten how to spell, and I am hoping she will soon forget how to write also."

MRS. CHRISTENSEN. The way you mimic people—I just have to laugh—although it's sinful.

[CHRISTENSEN *looks at his watch.*

RIIS. And they are not coming yet!—Will you go, or must I——?

MRS. RIIS. [*Rising*] I'll go. But they haven't had time yet——

RIIS. [*Close to his wife*] This is your fault! It's perfectly plain to me.

MRS. RIIS. I don't think you know what you are saying.

[*Goes out.*

RIIS. [*Coming back to the middle of the room*] I have to apologise—very much! This was the very last thing I should have expected of Svava. For I dare say that the laws of common courtesy have never before been violated in this house.

MRS. CHRISTENSEN. Something may have happened.

RIIS. Why, I never thought— Good God!

MRS. CHRISTENSEN. Don't misunderstand me now. I mean that a young girl is so sensitive to emotion—and then she hesitates to show herself.

RIIS. All the same, Mrs. Christensen, all the same! In a moment like this— Well, you must pardon me, but I cannot bear this. I simply must see for myself what is the matter.

[*He hurries out.*

CHRISTENSEN. If Alf had been here, I suppose he would also be running around the park after the lady.

MRS. CHRISTENSEN. But, dear!

CHRISTENSEN. Are we not alone?

MRS. CHRISTENSEN. Yes, but nevertheless——

CHRISTENSEN. Well, then I can only say as a famous man said long before me: Why the devil did he venture on board that galley?

MRS. CHRISTENSEN. Now be patient for a few moments! It's absolutely necessary.

CHRISTENSEN. Necessary? Pooh! Riis is more afraid of a breach than any one of us. Didn't you notice him a moment ago?

MRS. CHRISTENSEN. I did, but——

CHRISTENSEN. She has already gone far beyond what she has a right to.

MRS. CHRISTENSEN. That's what Alf thinks also.

CHRISTENSEN. Then he should have been on hand to say so. It was what I wanted.

MRS. CHRISTENSEN. Alf is in love—and that makes a man timid.

CHRISTENSEN. Oh-h!

MRS. CHRISTENSEN. Yes, being in love as often as you are is a different thing. [*She gets up*] There they come— No— not Svava!

CHRISTENSEN. Isn't she coming?

MRS. CHRISTENSEN. [*Speaking at the same time as her husband*] I don't see her.

RIIS. [*Appearing outside*] Here they are!

MRS. CHRISTENSEN. And your daughter?

RIIS. Svava, too! She just asked us to walk ahead. She wanted a chance to pull herself together.

MRS. CHRISTENSEN. [*Sitting down again*] There you see! It was as I thought.   Poor thing!

MRS. RIIS. Now she'll be here in a moment. [*Close to* MRS. CHRISTENSEN] You must forgive her—it has been a hard time for her.

MRS. CHRISTENSEN. Goodness gracious, I understand perfectly.   The first time you experience a thing of that kind, it's something dreadful.

CHRISTENSEN. Really, this is becoming quite amusing!

NORDAN. Now then! She just asked me to walk a little ahead.

RIIS. I think we have waited long enough.

NORDAN. She's right behind me.

RIIS. There she is!

> *Goes over toward the right;* MRS. RIIS *and* NORDAN
> *meet* SVAVA, *who is coming from the left.*

CHRISTENSEN. One might think it was the Queen of Sheba!

SIXTH SCENE

The same as before. SVAVA.   *Later* ALF.

SVAVA *has put on hat and gloves, and carries a parasol.*
MR. *and* MRS. CHRISTENSEN *have both stood up.   She
greets them with a slight movement of her head and walks
over to the corner on the right in the foreground.   Everybody sits down in silence;* NORDAN *furthest to the left;
then* MRS. RIIS, MRS. CHRISTENSEN, CHRISTENSEN;
and way over to the right, but in the background, RIIS,
who alternately sits down and gets up again.

MRS. CHRISTENSEN. My dear Svava, we have come here
to—well, you yourself know why.   What has happened has
caused us a great deal of sorrow.   But it's something that
cannot be undone.   We don't want to justify Alf's conduct.
But it seems to us he might be forgiven, particularly by one
who feels that she is loved, genuinely loved.   For that is
something entirely different!

CHRISTENSEN. Of course!

RIIS. Of course!

NORDAN. Of course!

CHRISTENSEN. And even if you don't agree to this, I hope
you can agree with regard to Alf himself.   For we believe,
my dear Svava, that in his character you have a guarantee
of absolute faithfulness.   I know that if it should be demanded
of him, he will give you his word of honour.

MRS. RIIS. [*Rising suddenly*] Oh, no, no!

MRS. CHRISTENSEN. What is it, my dear?

MRS. RIIS. Nothing of that kind!   Why, the marriage
ceremony itself is the same as a vow.

NORDAN. But perhaps two might be more effective, Mrs. Riis?

MRS. RIIS. No, not that!   No vows!   [*Sits down again.*

CHRISTENSEN. I have been noticing the remarks of our friend here, Dr. Nordan.—Tell me, my dear sir, do you also hold that my son's action must absolutely prevent his marriage with a respectable woman?

NORDAN. On the contrary!   Such a thing never prevents a man from marrying—and marrying very well at that.   So that in this case it is Svava alone who in every respect acts peculiarly.

MRS. CHRISTENSEN. I shouldn't say that.   But there is something Svava has overlooked.   She is acting as if she were free.   But she is far from free.   An engagement is a marriage. At least, I am old-fashioned enough to look at it that way. But then he to whom I have given my hand is also my lord, my master, and I owe it to him—as to everybody else in authority—to hold him in honour whether his actions be good or bad.   I cannot cast him aside or run away from him myself.

RIIS. That's old-fashioned and solid!   I thank you with all my heart, Mrs. Christensen!

NORDAN. I also——!

MRS. RIIS. But if it is too late *after* you are engaged——
                                          [*Checks herself.*

MRS. CHRISTENSEN. What do you mean, my dear?

MRS. RIIS. Oh, no—it wasn't anything at all.

NORDAN. If it is too late after the engagement, Mrs. Riis means—why not then tell the truth before the engagement?

RIIS. Well, there came the only thing still wanting!

CHRISTENSEN. Ah, but there would be style to that! Suppose hereafter a proposal should come to be something like this: "My dear young lady, up to date I have had so and so many love affairs—to wit, so and so many serious ones, and so and so many lighter ones." That would be an excellent introduction, wouldn't it, to——

NORDAN. ——to a declaration that he has never loved anybody else.

CHRISTENSEN. Not exactly that, but——

RIIS. Why, there's Alf!

MRS. RIIS. Alf?

MRS. CHRISTENSEN. Yes, there he is!

RIIS. [*Going to meet him*] That's right! I am glad to see you!

CHRISTENSEN. We-ell?

ALF. In the end I couldn't help myself. I had to come.

CHRISTENSEN. And right you did.

RIIS. It was the only natural thing.

> ALF *steps forward and bows very deeply to* SVAVA. *She acknowledges his greeting, but without looking at him. He steps back.*

NORDAN. Hello, my boy!

ALF. Perhaps my presence is not convenient?

RIIS. Far from it—on the contrary!

ALF. It seems, however, as if Miss Riis didn't wish to have me here?   [*Silence.*

MRS. CHRISTENSEN. But in a family conference like ours just now? Don't you think so, my dear?

RIIS. I assure you that you *are* welcome. It is just what you have to say that we are all waiting for.

CHRISTENSEN. That's right.

ALF. I have not succeeded in getting a hearing before now. I have repeatedly been turned away. Both I and my letters. And so I thought—that if I came now, I might be heard.

RIIS. Of course! Nobody would think of anything else.

NORDAN. You will be heard.

ALF. Perhaps I may regard Miss Riis's silence as a permission? In that case—well, it isn't much I have to say either. All I want is to recall the fact that when I applied for the hand of Miss Riis, I did so because I loved her with all my heart—her, and no one else. The greatest happiness I could imagine, and also the greatest honour, was to be loved by her in return. And nothing has changed since then.

> [*He makes a pause as if expecting an answer.*
> *Everybody looks at* SVAVA.

ALF. If Miss Riis expects me to say more than that—if she expects me to make apologies—well, I can't see the matter in that light. I can't feel myself under such an obligation to anybody. [*Silence*] What I might offer voluntarily—what I might be anxious to tell under other circumstances—of that I cannot speak now. But I am under no such obligation to anybody. My honour demands that I insist on this. The only thing for which I am responsible is my future. And in respect to that I must admit it has offended me deeply that Miss Riis has for a moment been able to doubt me. It has offended me very deeply. Never in my life have I been doubted in the same way before.—I must ask, with all proper respect, that I be taken at my word. [*After another pause*] Well, that's all.

MRS. RIIS. [*Rising instinctively*] But if under similar circumstances, a woman should say the same thing—who would believe her?

> *Silence.* SVAVA *bursts into tears.*

MRS. CHRISTENSEN. Poor child!

RIIS. Believe her?

MRS. RIIS. Yes, believe her.—Believe her if, with a past like that behind her, she dared to assert that she would always remain a faithful wife?

CHRISTENSEN. With such a past?

MRS. RIIS. Perhaps the expression is poor. But why demand that she trust the man more than he will trust her? For he wouldn't believe her at all.

RIIS. [*Coming up behind his wife*] Have you gone clear crazy?

CHRISTENSEN. [*Half rising*] If you pardon me, ladies and gentlemen, I think the two young people should be permitted to settle the matter.   [*Sits down again.*

ALF. I must confess that I have never given a thought to what Mrs. Riis is talking of, because it could never happen. No decent man would ever choose a woman of whose past he was not absolutely sure. Not one!

MRS. RIIS. But how about the decent woman, Alf?

ALF. That's a different thing.

NORDAN. To put it exactly: a woman owes the man both her past and her future, a man owes the woman only his future.

ALF. If you like—yes.

NORDAN. [*To* SVAVA, *as he gets up*] I did wish you to postpone your answer, Svava. But now I think you ought to answer at once.

> SVAVA *goes up to* ALF *and flings one of her gloves in his face. Then she disappears into her room.* ALF *makes a complete face-about to look after her.* RIIS *rushes into his room on the right. All are on their feet.* MRS. CHRISTENSEN *takes hold of* ALF'S *arm and goes out with him.* CHRISTENSEN *follows them.* MRS. RIIS *runs across the stage to the left.*

NORDAN. That was the gauntlet, all right.

MRS. RIIS. [*In front of the locked door behind which* SVAVA *has disappeared*] Svava!

CHRISTENSEN. [*Returns and says to* NORDAN *before the latter*

has noticed him or had a chance to turn around] It is war, then?
—Well, I think I know something about war! [*Goes out again.*
    NORDAN *turns around to look after him and remains
        standing that way.*
MRS. RIIS. [*At the door as before*] Svava!
    RIIS *comes out of his room in great haste, with hat and
        gloves on and a walking-stick in his hand; runs after
        the* CHRISTENSENS.
MRS. RIIS. Svava!

Curtain.

ACT III

A garden, at the end of which is seen the rear of a pretty one-story house.

FIRST SCENE

Nordan. Alf. Christensen.

Dr. Nordan *is sitting on a chair in the foreground, reading. An old man-servant opens the door of the house.*

Servant. Doctor!

Nordan. What is it? [Alf *appears in the door*] Oh, is it you? [*Rising*] Well, my boy?—But how you look!

Alf. Never mind that! Can you give me some breakfast?

Nordan. Have you had no breakfast yet? Haven't you been home? Not home all night? Not since yesterday? [*Calling out*] Thomas!

Alf. And when I have eaten, I must have a talk with you.

Nordan. Of course. My dear boy! [*To* Thomas] Get ready some breakfast in there.

[*Pointing to a window on the left side of the house.*

Alf. And I suppose I'll have to straighten out my appearance a little too?

Nordan. Go with Thomas! I'll be there in a moment. [Thomas *and* Alf *go into the house; at that moment a carriage is heard stopping in front of the house*] There is a carriage now! See what it is, Thomas!—No practice! Going away to-morrow!

Servant. It's Mr. Christensen, sir!   [*Goes out again.*

NORDAN. Ho-ho! [*Goes over to the window on the left*] Alf!

ALF. [*In the window*] Yes?

NORDAN. Your father! If you don't want to be seen, just pull down the shade.

The shade is drawn.

SERVANT. This way, please!

CHRISTENSEN. [*In evening dress; around his neck is seen the big cross worn by a Knight Commander of the Order of St. Olav; a light coat hangs across his shoulders*] I hope you will pardon me!

NORDAN. Certainly!—In all your glory?—Congratulations!

CHRISTENSEN. Oh, we freshly baked ones have to make our bow at court to-day. But on my way to the palace I thought I would stop for a moment with you, if you will let me.—Have you heard anything from that quarter? From the Riises?

NORDAN. No. I suppose they are waiting for the "war" to begin.

CHRISTENSEN. Well, it's coming! I intend to start it this very day. But I thought she might have become a little more reasonable? Women act ugly about that kind of thing as a rule. But afterward they become so much the meeker.

NORDAN. I don't think so. But I bow before your greater experience.

CHRISTENSEN. Thanks! But as a family buffer of long service, you must have a still greater.—Yesterday she was like an electric eel.—And she knew how to hit! I don't think the boy has been home ever since. I am almost glad of it. For it means there must be some shame in him. And I had almost begun to doubt it.

NORDAN. It is this matter about the "war" that interests *me*.

CHRISTENSEN. Oh, are you so keen on that? Well—I guess

that matter will take care of itself. The case of Mrs. North can be opened up again any day, my dear fellow. It rests with the bank, don't you know.

NORDAN. But what has it to do with your son's engagement?

CHRISTENSEN. What, you ask? My son is jilted by Miss Riis because she does not approve of his relations *before* the marriage. Her father maintains similar relations *in spite* of his marriage! *Tableau vivant très curieux*—to use the language of which Mr. Riis himself is so fond!

NORDAN. Oh, that's disgusting! For your son *alone* is to blame in this matter.

CHRISTENSEN. My son is not to blame at all. He has done nothing whatever that could bring harm or dishonour to the Riis family. Nothing whatsoever! He is an honest man who has given his promise to Miss Riis, and this promise he has kept. Who dares say anything else? Or that he does not *mean* to keep it? To doubt him is an insult, my dear doctor. There must be apologies—and peace—or war! For I am not going to stand this. And if my son intends to do so, I shall despise him.

NORDAN. *I* believe that your son's promise was honestly meant when he gave it. It is possible that he might have kept it also—but I don't know! I have learned to doubt. I am a physician. I have seen too much. And yesterday he did not appear to advantage.—Yes, you must pardon me. But on top of his lively bachelor life, and with the heritage that is back of him—if anybody doubted him—if his fiancée doubted him—do you really think that would be so very remarkable—my dear sir? Do you think he had a right to become offended? To demand apologies? Apologies for what? Because somebody dared to doubt his virtue?—Just think of it!

CHRISTENSEN. Oh, fiddlesti——

NORDAN. One moment! I am only half through. For you spoke also of peace—which means marriage. And if your son cares to marry a woman who does not feel sure of him, then *I* shall despise him.

CHRISTENSEN. Well——!

NORDAN. Well, I shall. That shows how opinions may differ. According to the way I feel about it, your son has simply to submit—and to wait. Wait and keep quiet. Always provided, of course, that he is still in love.—Now you know what I think of the matter.

CHRISTENSEN. First of all I presume that most suitors have erred in the same way as my son. At least, that is my own belief. Furthermore I presume that they have the same unfortunate "heritage"—a word on which you lay especial emphasis out of friendly consideration for me. But is that any reason for a majority of engaged young women to behave as Miss Riis does? To raise an outcry, to run away, to make a scandal? If it were, what a hubbub there would be! The result would be the most diverting anarchy ever heard of in this world— No, these doctrines now confronting us are against the nature and order of things. They are false. And when, in the bargain, they are hurled at our heads in the form of judgments by a Supreme Court of Morals, then I strike back! Good-bye! [*Starts to leave, but turns back*] Against *whom* would these Supreme Court decisions be directed, do you think? As a rule, against the best and ablest young men in the country. And *these* are the men that we should put in a class by themselves as special objects of derision!—And against *what* would those decisions turn? Against the better part of the world's literature and art; against a great deal of what is most beautiful, most entrancing in our own time—above all, against the great cities of the world. Against those world-miracles—the cities of vast

millions. You cannot deny it!—Just that life which keeps
apart from marriage, or breaks it up, or tries to change the
whole institution—yes, you know very well what I mean—
all that which we describe as "seductive" in fashions, in
luxury, in sociability, in art, in literature—it is just this
which contributes more than anything else to the richness of
life in the big cities. It is one of their main sources of power.
Nobody who has seen it, can doubt this. But everybody
pretends not to understand. Is then all this to be destroyed?
Are the best among our youths to be made outcasts? Are
the great cities of the world to be ruined?—Yes, people demand so much in the name of morality, that at last they
demand what is immoral.

NORDAN. Ah, you are, indeed, applying the superior ability
of a statesman to your little war.

CHRISTENSEN. Nothing but common sense, my dear fellow.
But that's all that's needed. And you may be sure that the
whole city will be on my side.

SERVANT. Doctor!

NORDAN. Well, I declare!   [*He hurries toward the house.*

SECOND SCENE

The same as before. MRS. RIIS.

MRS. RIIS. May I come in?

NORDAN. Of course you may!

MRS. RIIS [*To* CHRISTENSEN, *who has saluted her*] My visit
is really for you.

CHRISTENSEN. I am delighted!

MRS. RIIS. I happened to be at the window just as your
carriage drove up and you stepped out. And so I thought I
should seize the opportunity—for yesterday you uttered a

threat against us. Am I right? You declared war against us?

CHRISTENSEN. It seems to me that it was declared, and that I merely accepted it?

MRS. RIIS. And what is the object of your war, if I may ask?

CHRISTENSEN. I have just explained my position to the doctor. But I doubt whether it would be chivalrous to do so to you.

NORDAN. Then I shall do it. The war is directed against your husband. Mr. Christensen means to take the offensive.

MRS. RIIS. Of course! For you know that you can reach him. But I have come to ask you to reconsider.

CHRISTENSEN. [*Smiling*] Is that so?

MRS. RIIS. Once—it is many years ago now—I picked up my child in my arms and meant to leave my husband. Then he mentioned a name. He used it as a shield. It was the name of a very powerful man. And he said: "Observe how forbearing that man's wife is. And because of her, the whole community is forbearing. And those who will benefit by it are their children."—Those were his exact words.

CHRISTENSEN. Well? In so far as advice was suggested, it was good advice. And you took it, didn't you?

MRS. RIIS. In our country it is a shame to be a divorced wife. And it brings no honour to be the daughter of such a woman. The wealthy, the powerful people, those that set the tone, have caused it to be so.

CHRISTENSEN. Oh, well——?

MRS. RIIS. This was my excuse when I stayed for the sake of my child's future. But it was also my husband's excuse —he being one who follows the example set by others.

CHRISTENSEN. We all do, madam.

MRS. RIIS. But the men of most power less than others.

And in this respect they are setting examples which are very tempting to the rest.—I can hardly be mistaken in assuming that, during these last days, I have heard *your* ideas from my husband's lips. But if mistaken in this, I was surely right in hearing *you* back of what your son said yesterday?

CHRISTENSEN. I stand by every word my son spoke.

MRS. RIIS. So I thought. Well, it will be a strange war, this one of yours. For you are back of everything that has happened from first to last. You are the whole war—on both sides.

NORDAN. Before you answer!—May I submit to you, Mrs. Riis, whether you want to make the breach incurable? Is a conciliation between the two young people to be rendered impossible?

MRS. RIIS. It *is* impossible.

NORDAN. Why?

MRS. RIIS. Because all confidence is gone.

NORDAN. Now any more than before?

MRS. RIIS. Yes, for I must confess that until yesterday, when Alf's word of honour was offered—and until he himself demanded that he be trusted on his word of honour—until then I had not recognised my own story. And yet, that's what it was—*word for word!* That's the way we began! Who can guarantee that the sequel will not be the same?

CHRISTENSEN. My son's character is a guarantee of that, madam.

MRS. RIIS. Character?—Yes, you think that a character is developed by following secret, lawless ways from youth up! But that is the way to develop faithlessness. And those who complain that real characters are so rare, should seek the cause right here, I think.

CHRISTENSEN. It is not one's youth that determines the matter. What settles it is how one marries.

Mrs. Riis. Why should faithlessness cease with marriage? Can you tell me that?

Christensen. Because then there is love.

Mrs. Riis. Then there is love? As if there had been no love before!—It is just in this respect that the men have fostered a complete delusion. No, love cannot bring lasting faith when the will itself is impaired. And it is. Impaired through the life the bachelor leads.

Christensen. And yet I know very sensual men with strong wills.

Mrs. Riis. I am not talking of strong wills, but of clean ones. Of loyal and noble wills.

Christensen. If my son is to be condemned by that kind of nonsense, then I praise the Lord that he got away before it was too late. Yes, I do!—And this will be enough!

[*Starts to go.*

Mrs. Riis. As to your son—? Doctor, tell me—and so that his father may hear it before he leaves—that time when you refused to come to the engagement party, had you already heard something about Alf Christensen? And was what you had heard of such a nature that you couldn't trust him?

Nordan. [*After a moment's hesitation*] No, not exactly!

Mrs. Riis. Do you hear that?—But then I must ask you, doctor: why didn't you say anything? Why, in the name of God, did you keep silent?

Nordan. Listen, Mrs. Riis; when two young people, who at bottom suit each other—for they do, don't they?

Christensen. Yes, they do—I admit that.

Nordan. When they all at once fall insanely in love with each other—what can a man do?

Christensen. Oh, he can manufacture stories, exaggerations, scandals!

NORDAN. And then I must confess—as I think I have said before—that I have grown accustomed to the fact that things in this respect are not as they should be—I looked upon this engagement as upon others—as upon most of them—as a lottery. It might come out well; it might turn out badly.

MRS. RIIS. And my daughter, of whom you are fond—for I know you are—her you would stake in a lottery! Could anything give a better idea of how matters stand?

NORDAN. Yes, there is something—for you yourself, Mrs. Riis—what did you do?

MRS. RIIS. I?

CHRISTENSEN. Good!

NORDAN. *You* learned also what Hoff had told—and more besides.

CHRISTENSEN *laughs in a subdued way.*

NORDAN. And yet you helped your husband—if not to make Svava overlook the whole thing, at least in trying to smooth it over.

CHRISTENSEN. Bravo!

NORDAN. And you called me in to assist you in getting more time.

CHRISTENSEN. In matters like these, you know, the mothers distinguish to some extent between theory and practice.

NORDAN. It was only when I saw Svava—how deeply she took it, and how she had come to fear it—that my own eyes were opened. And I listened to her until my sympathy became aroused. I, too, was young once, and believed—and loved. But all that happened so long ago. And I have grown so tired——

MRS. RIIS. [*Who in the meantime has seated herself at* DR. NORDAN's *small reading table*] Oh, God!

NORDAN. Yes, Mrs. Riis, let me be quite frank about it: it is just the mothers who have gradually blunted my feelings. Because they themselves don't seem to care.—And as a rule they are perfectly aware of what they are dealing with.

CHRISTENSEN. They are, my dear fellow, they are! And Mrs. Riis is no exception. For you must admit, madam, that you, in your time, did your best to hang on to a young man with a pretty lively past!—And for that matter, he held a fine position socially, that young man—something I mention quite incidentally.

NORDAN. Oh, well, well!—But no sooner have the daughters a chance to make what their mothers call a "good marriage," than the old ones forget their own sufferings.

MRS. RIIS. But we don't know that it is the same thing over again.

NORDAN. You don't know?

MRS. RIIS. I tell you that I didn't realise it. We always believe that the men chosen by our daughters are so much better. We believe the guarantees to be better, the conditions to be changed. And it *is* so! It is a sort of mirage that deludes us.

CHRISTENSEN. Through the expectation of a good marriage —yes! I quite agree with you, madam, for the first time. Otherwise I have an idea that all this proves something else, too. Perhaps, after all, the women don't suffer so much by the fact that men are men? How is that? Perhaps the trouble is more violent than deep-going—something like seasickness? When it's over—well, then it is over. And when the time comes for the daughters to board the ship, their dear mammas think: oh, well, they'll bear it as we did. Only get them started! For they want so badly to see them started—that's the whole trouble!

MRS. RIIS. [*As she gets up and moves toward the foreground*] Well, if it be so, then it is nothing to laugh at! For then it proves to what depth a woman may sink through her life in common with a man.

CHRISTENSEN. Well, I'll——!

MRS. RIIS. Yes, for every new generation of women comes with a stronger and stronger demand for a decent life. The mere sense of motherhood is enough to develop that demand. It is meant for a protection to those that cannot protect themselves. Even bad mothers have the feeling of it. And if, nevertheless, they surrender, and if each new generation of women sinks as deeply in marriage as you say, then this must be caused by the special privilege which man asserts. For it is this privilege which has developed him.

CHRISTENSEN. Which special privilege?

MRS. RIIS. That of living as he pleases while still unmarried, and of being taken on his word of honour when he chooses to enter marriage. As long as woman cannot stop this dreadful privilege, or make herself independent of it—so long will one half of mankind remain a victim of the other half—of that other half's lack of self-control. This one privilege has proved itself stronger than all the work ever done for freedom on this earth. And that is nothing to laugh at.

CHRISTENSEN. You are dreaming of another world than ours, madam, and of natures different from ours. And, of course—if you pardon me!—therein lies the only answer needed.

MRS. RIIS. Why don't you then give the same answer in public? Why don't you step forth into full daylight and acknowledge your views?

CHRISTENSEN. Are we not doing so?

MRS. RIIS. No—not in this country. On the contrary! For publicly you place yourself under *our* flag, while secretly you desert it. Why have you not the courage to unfold a flag of your own? Let those bachelor habits be established as quite proper! Then the fight will begin at last. And then each innocent bride may at last know where she is going—and in what capacity.

NORDAN. That means the abolition of marriage—nothing more or less.

MRS. RIIS. Well, wouldn't that be better? For now it's being destroyed—long before it is begun!

CHRISTENSEN. Yes, and the man is at fault, of course. That's the fashion nowadays. It's part of the "work of emancipation." His authority must go!

MRS. RIIS. The one he has gained during his life as bachelor.

NORDAN. Ha, ha!

MRS. RIIS. Don't let us cover up the thing with phrases. Let us rather speak of what the poet has called "the blighting of the hearth." For what it means is just blighted marriages. And whence does it spring—this chilling, gruesome materialism, this pleasure-craving brutality? Where does it come from?—I might describe something that lies still nearer at hand. But I won't. I shall not even mention the prevalent family diseases.—But drag it out into the open! Perhaps then it will break into flames, too. And our consciences will be smitten by it! And it will become the most important matter of all in every home! *This* is what is wanted!

CHRISTENSEN. Now we have worked ourselves up to such an elevation that it doesn't sound impressive at all when I say that I am expected in certain "very exalted" quarters. But nevertheless you'll have to excuse me.

MRS. RIIS. I hope I haven't delayed you.

CHRISTENSEN. No, there is plenty of time. I am only longing—please, don't take it badly—to get away from here.

MRS. RIIS. To your—equals?

CHRISTENSEN. I am glad you remind me of them. It

makes me realise that I shall probably not have to meet you or yours any more?

MRS. RIIS. No, you have received your dismissal from us.

CHRISTENSEN. Well, thank heaven! Now I only hope to be able to distribute the ridicule in accordance with justice.

MRS. RIIS. To do so, you need only publish your autobiography.

CHRISTENSEN. No, rather your family principles, madam! For they are really too funny for anything. And when I describe the way they are put into practice within the family itself, I have reason to think that people will laugh rather heartily. Or to speak seriously: I'll get after your husband in his reputation and in his business, until he has to leave the city. I am not going to accept a humiliation like this without paying back in equal coin.   [*Starts to leave.*

NORDAN. But this is revolting!

ALF. [*Appears in the doorway of the house*] Father!

CHRISTENSEN. You here?—And how badly you look! Where have you been, my boy?

ALF. I got here just ahead of you, and I have heard everything. I may as well tell you at once, that if you begin that kind of warfare, then I'll go around everywhere telling why Miss Riis broke her engagement with me.—I'll tell it just as it is.—Yes, you can sneer at me as much as you please. But I'll do it. And I shall begin at once.

CHRISTENSEN. I think you can save yourself the trouble. After the breach your reputation will probably travel a great deal more quickly than yourself.

NORDAN. [*Goes over to* ALF] To be plain, Alf: do you still love her?

ALF. You ask because you think she has wronged me? But now I understand why she did it—and why she *had* to do it. Now I understand!

CHRISTENSEN. And forgive her?   Without further ado?

ALF. I love her more than ever—and no matter what she thinks of me.

CHRISTENSEN. Well, well, well!—Then there is nothing more to say about it.   You insist on your right to play the part of lover—and to us self-respecting people you leave nothing but to grin and bear your bad acting as we may best. —I suppose you'll go right over and pay your duty call on account of yesterday's festivities?   And ask for a respite till to-morrow?   While, with as much haste as propriety will permit, you hurry through some kind of purgatory?   May I ask the location of that institution and its methods?—No, my boy, don't get melodramatic!   When you can stand what you got from that little Riis girl yesterday and from her mother to-day, then you can also stand a few gibes and prods from your own father.   I have had to stand the whole engagement, and the breach, too!   And being sprinkled with moral waters on top of it!   Oh, damn it all!   I hope I don't stink of the thing when I get up to the palace!   [*He goes toward the house.   In the doorway he turns about for a moment*] Your travelling money will be waiting for you at the office. [*Goes out.*

NORDAN. Does that mean another exile?

ALF. Of course!   [*He shows great excitement.*

MRS. RIIS. Now you'll have to come over with me, doctor, and that at once!

NORDAN. How is she taking it?

MRS. RIIS. I don't know.

NORDAN. You don't know?

MRS. RIIS. Yesterday she wanted to be alone.   This morning she left the house very early.

NORDAN. Then something must have happened?

MRS. RIIS. Yes.   You said yesterday that you had given her a hint about—about her father.

NORDAN. And then?

MRS. RIIS. Then I felt that the time to keep silent was over.

NORDAN. And you——?

MRS. RIIS. I have written to her.

NORDAN. Written?

MRS. RIIS. It came more naturally. Then we didn't have to talk it over. I wrote, and tore up—and wrote again. The whole afternoon yesterday and all night. Wrote! There wasn't much of it. But it came hard.

NORDAN. And now she has got it?

MRS. RIIS. This morning, when she had eaten and was starting out, I sent it after her.—And now, dearest friend, I want *you* to come and talk to her. And then you tell me when I can come. For I am afraid! [*She covers up her face.*

NORDAN. I saw, the moment you came in, that something important had happened. And you were so hot-headed!— Good God, how this thing has spread and grown!

MRS. RIIS. You shouldn't go away, doctor! Don't go away from her now!

NORDAN. Oh, that's what it was!—Thomas!

SERVANT. Yes, sir!

NORDAN. You don't have to pack.

SERVANT. Not pack!—Your stick, sir!

[*Handing* NORDAN *his walking-stick.*

NORDAN. Will you take my arm, madam?

The SERVANT *opens the door for them.*

ALF. [*Stepping forward*] Mrs. Riis!—Will you let me speak to her?

MRS. RIIS. Speak to her?—Oh, that's out of the question!

NORDAN. Why, you heard yourself what she has to think of to-day.

Mrs. Riis. And if she didn't want to speak to you before, she certainly will not do so now.

Alf. When she asks for permission to see me, will you then tell her that I am here? And I'll stay here till she asks!

Mrs. Riis. But what's the use of it?

Alf. Well, that's our concern. I know that she wants to speak to me.—Just tell her that I am here! That's all that's needed! [*He walks away and disappears in the garden.*

Nordan. He doesn't know what he is saying.

Mrs. Riis. Let us be going, doctor—I am afraid!

Nordan. And so am I!—Hm—so now she knows *that!*

[*They go out.*

ACT IV

Same room as in the first two acts.

FIRST SCENE

Svava. Dr. Nordan.

Svava *comes in, walking very slowly; looks around the
room; goes up to the door and steps outside for a moment; comes back into the room; when she turns around
again,* Dr. Nordan *is standing in the doorway.*

Svava. Is that *you—?* Oh, Uncle Nordan!   [*She sobs.*
Nordan. My dear—dear little girl!   Now be brave!

Svava. But haven't you seen mother?   They said she had
gone over to you?

Nordan. She will be here in a moment.—But, do you
know—we two ought to take a long walk instead of talking
with your mother or anybody else.   A long, quiet walk?
What do you say?

Svava. No, I cannot do that.

Nordan. Why?

Svava. Because I must get through with it.

Nordan. What do you mean?

Svava. [*Paying no attention to his question*] Uncle——

Nordan. Yes.

Svava. Does Alf know this?   Did he, too, know it?

Nordan. Yes.

Svava. Of course, everybody but me.   Oh, I have such a
longing to hide myself—hide myself!   And that's what I am
going to do.—Now I can see things as they are.   There is a

93

big mountain against which I have put my hands to push it away. And the others have stood around laughing at me. —But I want to speak with Alf.

NORDAN. With Alf?

SVAVA. I behaved very unwisely yesterday. I should never have gone in. But you just carried me along. I hardly knew that I went with you.

NORDAN. Then it was that about your father—what I said about your father—that——

SVAVA. I didn't understand at once. But when I was alone —mother's peculiar anxiety, my father's threat to leave the country, all sorts of remarks and symptoms—so many, many things that I had not understood, or hardly even noticed— and all at once—they were there!—I pushed the thing away from me, and it came back.—It came back, and it came back! —And then it was as if every limb of mine had been lamed. —When you took hold of my arm and said, now you *must* come in—at that moment I could hardly think at all. Everything was in a whirl!

NORDAN. Well, I acted like a big fool—and twice in succession at that!

SVAVA. No, it was better. Much better. Of course, it didn't come about in the right way. I must speak to Alf. For it mustn't remain that way.—But otherwise it was better. And now I must get through with it.

NORDAN. What do you mean by that?

SVAVA. Where is mother?

NORDAN. My dear girl, you shouldn't do anything to-day. Better not speak to anybody at all. If you do—well, I don't know what may happen.

SVAVA. But I know.—Yes, it's of no use!—You think I am all nerves to-day? Well, so I am. But if you oppose me, it will only get worse.

NORDAN. I don't oppose you either. All I want——

SVAVA. Yes, yes, yes!—But where *is* mother?—And *you* have to get hold of Alf! I couldn't go to him—could I? Or do you think he is too proud to come here after what happened yesterday? Oh, no, that isn't like Alf! And tell him that he must not be too proud toward one who has been so humiliated.

[*She cries.*

NORDAN. But do you really think you can——?

SVAVA. Oh, you don't know what I can do. Only I must get through with this. For it has lasted long enough now.

NORDAN. I have to ask your mother, then——?

SVAVA. Yes—and Alf?

NORDAN. Yes, after a while. But if you——

SVAVA. No—no "but!"

NORDAN. And if you need me, I shall not go away until you are "through," as you call it.

SVAVA *runs up to him and puts her arms around him.* DR. NORDAN *goes out.*

SECOND SCENE

SVAVA. *A little later* MRS. RIIS.

MRS. RIIS. [*Approaching* SVAVA] My child! [*Stops still.*

SVAVA. Yes, mother, I cannot meet you—my whole body is shaking. And don't you know what it is? Has it not occurred to you that you cannot treat me like that?

MRS. RIIS. Treat you, Svava?

SVAVA. Heavens, mother! That you let me live day after day, year after year—without letting me know what kind of thing I was living with? To let me preach the most extreme principles in a house like ours?

MRS. RIIS. But you didn't want me to tell my own child that——?

SVAVA. Not while I was still a child! But when I grew up? Yes, by all means! Hadn't I a right to choose whether or no I wanted to stay in such a home? Hadn't I a right to know what is known to everybody else—or what they might learn at any minute?

MRS. RIIS. I have never thought of it in that way.

SVAVA. Never thought of it in that way? Mother!

MRS. RIIS. Never! To spare you; to keep peace in our home—while you were a child; and later, to let nothing interfere with your studies, your interests, your pleasures—for you are not like others, Svava!—to do that I have watched with the utmost care lest any such knowledge reach you.   I thought it my duty!   You have no idea of how far I have stooped in order to—for your sake, child!

SVAVA. But you had no right to do so, mother!

MRS. RIIS. No right——?

SVAVA. No! For when you lowered yourself for my sake, you lowered me, too!

MRS. RIIS. [*Deeply moved*] Good God, Svava——!

SVAVA. Why, I am not reproaching you, mother!—Dear mother, I wouldn't do that for anything in the world!—It only makes me so inexpressibly sad, so shocked—for your sake—that you could be carrying within you such a secret! Never for a moment dare to be yourself with me! Always something to hide!   And that you could hear me praise what was not worthy of praise—that you could see me trust— could see me give my love to—oh, mother, mother, mother!

MRS. RIIS. Yes, I have felt it that way myself.   Oh, yes! A thousand times! But I didn't think I could dare! Oh, it was wrong—wrong! Now I see! But would you have had me go my own way the moment I myself found out?

Svava. That's more than I dare to answer. You have settled that yourself. Every one must settle that—in accordance with her own strength and the strength of her love. But when it kept on until I was grown up—! And that's the reason, of course, why I made a second mistake! I was brought up to be mistaken.

> Riis *is heard humming a song as he approaches from the left.*

Mrs. Riis. Merciful heavens, there he is!

Riis. [*Is seen passing the left-hand window in the background, but at the door he stops and exclaims*] Oh, that's right!

> [*Then he turns and walks away hurriedly.*

Mrs. Riis. But, child, what a changed look came over you! Svava, you frighten me! You cannot mean to——

Svava. But what have you been thinking, mother?

Mrs. Riis. That I have stood so much for your sake, that you, perhaps, might stand a little for my sake.

Svava. Of this? Not in the least!

Mrs. Riis. But what do you want to do?

Svava. Go away from here, of course!

Mrs. Riis. [*Utters a cry*] —Then I go with you!

Svava. You? Go away from father?

Mrs. Riis. It is for your sake I have stayed with him. Without you, not a single day— Oh, *you don't want me!*

Svava. Mother, dear!—I must get accustomed to all that's new to me. Even you seem new to me. And, of course, I have been mistaken about you also.—I must be by myself.— Oh, now, don't get so miserable!

Mrs. Riis. This on top of all! O God, this on top of the rest!

Svava. Mother dear—I cannot do otherwise. Now I shall give myself wholly to my kindergartens. I must, I must!

And if I am not permitted to be alone, I shall go still farther
away.

Mrs. Riis. This is the worst of all! This is the worst!—
There I hear—yes, it's him! Don't say anything now!
More than this I cannot endure! Not all at once!—Try to
be kind, Svava! Do you hear?

> *Humming as before,* Riis *comes again, but now with an
> overcoat carried over his arm.* Svava *rushes toward
> the foreground; after a moment's wavering, she sits
> down far over to the left, with her back turned toward
> the centre of the room so that she appears in half profile
> to the audience; she looks nervously for something with
> which she can seem occupied.*

THIRD SCENE

Svava. Mrs. Riis. Riis. *Later* Alf.

Riis. [*Puts the overcoat on a chair; he is in full dress and
wears the badge of St. Olav*] Good morning, ladies, good morning!

Mrs. Riis. Good morning.

Riis. First big news item: with whom did I drive from the
palace?—Christensen!

Mrs. Riis. Really?

Riis. The thundering Jove of yesterday—exactly! With
him and my brother the Director-General. And I was the
first one he shook hands with when he arrived at the palace.
He made conversation with me, he introduced me to people
—a regular exhibition it was!

Mrs. Riis. Well!

Riis. Of course, nothing happened yesterday. Nowhere
in the world was any gauntlet thrown—least of all in the face

of his first-born! Christensen, the worshipful Knight Commander of to-day's make, has a longing for peace. In the end we had a glass of champagne together at my brother's.

MRS. RIIS. That was very nice.

RIIS. Therefore: be in good spirits, ladies! Nothing has happened. Absolutely nothing. We'll begin the feast all over again, with a fresh, clean table-cloth, on which not a single drop has been spilled.

MRS. RIIS. That's very fortunate.

RIIS. Yes, isn't it? Our dear daughter's rather violent discharge of electricity has relieved her own mind and cleared up the ideas of other people—the air is now agreeably refreshing, not to say fecund.

MRS. RIIS. And at the palace? How was it?

RIIS. Well, my dear—looking around at our little group of fresh-baked worthies, I dared not persuade myself that virtue is the thing rewarded in this world. However, some sort of solemn proclamation was spread before us. There was something we should save—it must have been the State, now I think of it—or perhaps it was the Church? Well, I don't know, for I didn't read it. But everybody signed.

MRS. RIIS. You also?

RIIS. I also! Why not keep in good company? Up there, on life's mountain tops, one gets a more pleasing, a more untrammelled view of life. Up there, all are friends. They came and congratulated me—and in the end I couldn't make out whether it was on my own behalf or that of my daughter. Nor did I know that I had so many friends here in the city, not to say at Court. But in such glorious company, and in an atmosphere laden with praise and flattery and pleasantries, what's the use of examining things too closely? And then, nothing but men, just men! There is after all—if the ladies will pardon me—something charming at times to be surrounded only by men, by men in a festive mood. The conversation becomes a little more highly spiced, more to the point, more full-blooded, and the laughter much more hearty. One understands one another almost before the word is spoken.

MRS. RIIS. You seem very happy to-day?

RIIS. Yes, so I am, and no mistake! And I should like everybody else to be happy also. Of course, life could be a great deal better; but when you see it from those heights, you know also that it might be much worse. And as far as we men are concerned—well, we have our faults. But at bottom we are awfully amusing. And I bet you, life would be pretty tedious without us.—Let us then take life as it is, my dear, darling Svava! [*As he goes toward her, she rises*] What is this? Are you still in a bad humour? After having slapped him in the face with your own glove, and in full family council at that? Can you reasonably ask more of life? I think you ought to be laughing aloud— Or is something the matter? What? Oh, what is it now again?

MRS. RIIS. It is——

RIIS. It is——?

MRS. RIIS. Oh, it is— Alf will be here in a moment!

RIIS. Here? Alf? In a moment? Hooray! Then I understand! But why didn't you tell me at once?

MRS. RIIS. You have been talking ever since you came in.

RIIS. Yes, I think I have! Well, even if *you* take it seriously, my dear Svava, I hope you won't object to your "noble" papa taking it humorously? For it does amuse me extremely. My spirits went up the moment I guessed from Christensen's manner that everything was all right. And now Alf will be here in a moment? Then I understand everything. Once more: hooray! Why, this is after all the finest thing that has happened so far to-day! I feel as if I

simply *had* to accompany his entrance with a triumphal overture.   [*He goes humming toward the piano.*

MRS. RIIS. Oh, no, dear! Please, don't!

> RIIS *begins to play as if he didn't hear her;* MRS. RIIS
> *goes over to him and stops him, pointing at the same
> time to* SVAVA.

SVAVA. Let him play! Just let him play, dear! This inno-
cent gaiety which has amused me ever since I was a child—
[*She breaks into tears, but checks herself quickly*] Disgusting!
Horrible!

RIIS. You look as if you wanted to throw more gloves
to-day. So it isn't over yet?

SVAVA. No, it isn't.

RIIS. Perhaps you want to borrow mine, if your own
shouldn't——

MRS. RIIS. No—not that way!

SVAVA. Yes, that way, too. Let him mock at us! One
possessing his moral resolution ought to mock at us.

RIIS. What do you mean by that? Do you call it lack of
moral resolution that I don't care for old maids or sour-faced
virtue?

SVAVA. Father—you are——!

MRS. RIIS. Oh, Svava!

RIIS. No, let her finish! It is quite a novel sensation to
see a well-bred girl throw gloves in the face of her fiancé and
innuendoes in the face of her father!—Especially when it is
done for morality's sake!

SVAVA. Don't mention morality! Or do so to Mrs. North!

RIIS. Mrs.—Mrs.— What has she got——?

SVAVA. Oh, be quiet! I know everything you have——

MRS. RIIS. Svava!

SVAVA. That's right!—For mother's sake we'll go no further!—But when, yesterday, I threw that glove of which you

have so much to say, I knew this.   And that's why I did it!
It was meant for everything of this kind, for the beginning
and the continuation, for him and for you!   Then I understood your righteous zeal in this matter—as well as the moral
indignation which you showed and voiced to mother.

Mrs. Riis. Svava!

Svava. Oh, that politeness of yours, that concern for
mother which I have so often admired—and your jests, your
good-humour, your elegance—I have just learned what it all
means!—No, no, I can no longer believe in anything!   Oh,
it's horrible, horrible!

Mrs. Riis. But, Svava!

Svava. All life has become unclean to me.   The nearest
and dearest has been blackened.   And for that reason I feel
it since yesterday as if I had been made an outcast.   And
what else am I?   Cast out from all that I loved and treasured,
and this without any fault of my own!   And yet, what I feel
most, is not pain.   No, it is humiliation, shame.   All that I
have dared to say is now turned into words merely—and all
that I have dared to do on my own behalf is nothing but big
words—and this without any fault of my own!   For it is
your fault!—I thought I knew something about life.   But I
was to learn a lot more.   I suppose the meaning of it was to
make me stoop so low that at last I should fit into it.—Now,
and now only, has it become clear to me what you were
teaching me all the time—while you appealed to God and to
my mother for support.   But it was all of no use!—It is a
great deal, I should say, to live through the thoughts I have
had to face, yesterday, last night, to-day.   But once done, it
is done for ever.   Afterward there is nothing that can surprise!—Oh, that a man has the heart to let his own child live
through such a thing!

Mrs. Riis. Look at your father!

SVAVA. Yes—if you find what I say to you very hard—then remember what I used to say to you. Not longer ago than yesterday morning, on this very spot. Then you have a measure of what I have thought of you, father—and of what, because of it, I now feel in *here!*—Oh——!

RIIS. Svava!

SVAVA. You have ruined my home for me. The very memory of the time spent in it is spoiled. And I cannot think of it as a home for the future either.

RIIS *and* MRS. RIIS. But, Svava!

SVAVA. No, I cannot! All sense of security is gone! And then it is no longer a home. Since yesterday I am a tenant only.

RIIS. My child—don't say that!

SVAVA. Yes, I am your child. You have only to say it as you did now, and I feel it deeply. And all we have lived together, we two! All the fun we have had on our travels; all that we have read together, played together—now it cannot even be remembered—I cannot go back to it in my mind! And that is why I cannot stay here!

RIIS. You cannot stay here?

SVAVA. No, it would remind me of too many things—all of which are now spoiled.

MRS. RIIS. And you'll see that it is just as hard to leave.

RIIS. But—*I* can go!

MRS. RIIS. You?

RIIS. And you can stay here with your mother. But—Svava——?

SVAVA. No, I cannot accept that—no matter what happens——

RIIS. Don't say anything more! I beg you, Svava! Don't make me too, too miserable! Remember that not until to-day— Never have I dreamt of making you— If you cannot endure me any longer—if you cannot—then let me go away. It is I—who am the guilty one. Svava, don't you hear? I, not you! You must stay here!

MRS. RIIS. Mercy, there is Alf!

RIIS. Alf! [Silence.

ALF. [Stops in the doorway; pause] Perhaps I had better leave again——?

RIIS. Leave again?—Leave again, you say?—By no means! Oh, no!—You couldn't come more conveniently! Really, you couldn't! Dear fellow—my dear fellow, let me thank you!

MRS. RIIS. [To SVAVA] Do you want to be left alone?

SVAVA. No, no, no!

RIIS. You want to speak to Svava, do you?—I think the most proper thing I can do is to retire. You two ought to have a chance to talk it out. Be by yourselves. Yes, of course! And with your permission, I'll disappear. You don't mind? I have really some very important business in the city. You must pardon me! I am only going to make a quick change. Pardon! [Goes into his room.

ALF. Of course, I can come some other time.

MRS. RIIS. But you want badly to have a talk with her at once?

ALF. There can be no question here of what I want. I can see—and Dr. Nordan told me—that Miss Riis has been under a great strain. But I thought it my duty to come just the same.

SVAVA. And I thank you for it. It is more—much more than I have deserved. But I want to tell you at once that what happened yesterday—I mean, the way it happened— the reason of it was that I had just learned something I had never known before. And all was mixed in my mind.

[She can no longer hide her emotion.

ALF. I knew that what happened yesterday—you would regret to-day. I know how kind you are. And in that lay my one hope of seeing you again.

RIIS. [*Comes from his room, having partly changed his dress*] If anybody wants anything done in the city—I'll attend to it—no? I have thought that the ladies might like a trip abroad. How does it strike you? When one's thoughts are about to become—what shall I say?—too severe, or rather, too heavy—it offers a remarkable diversion. I have often noticed it myself. Oh, quite often!—Think it over, will you?—I might as well make arrangements at once, if perchance—how about it? Well: good-bye for a while! And think it over! I myself think it would be fine.

> *Goes out through the door in the background and turns to the left.*

> SVAVA *looks smilingly at her mother for a moment; then she hides her face in her hands.*

MRS. RIIS. If you don't mind for a moment, I must——

SVAVA. Mother!

MRS. RIIS. I cannot help it, child. I must try to calm down a little. And I shall only be in there. [*Pointing toward the room on the left*] And soon I shall be here again.   [*Goes out.*

> SVAVA *sinks down on a chair by the table, wholly overcome by her emotion.*

FOURTH SCENE

SVAVA. ALF.

ALF. Now I have a feeling that the whole matter has come back to us two.

SVAVA. Yes——

ALF. I suppose you know that since yesterday I have done

nothing but make up speeches to you?—But now that doesn't help me a bit.

SVAVA. But it was kind of you to come.

ALF. Let me then ask just one thing of you—but that one I ask with my whole heart: *wait for me!*—For now I know what road leads up to you.   We had laid out a plan of life, we two, and although I shall be alone about it now—I want to carry that plan through!   And I shall!   And then, perhaps, some day, when you see how faithful I have been—? I have been ordered not to bother you, and least of all to-day. But let me have an answer—quietly, very quietly.   Won't you?

SVAVA. But why?

ALF. I need it to live on.   For I am one of those men to whom life means the more the higher hangs the prize.—An answer!

SVAVA. [*Tries to speak, but bursts into tears*] You see, everything upsets me to-day.   I cannot.—And what do you want? That I shall wait?   What does it mean?   To be through— and yet not through;   try to forget—and yet build up new hope. [*Again overcome by her feelings*] No!

ALF. I can see that you ought to be left alone.   And yet it is impossible for me to leave.

> SVAVA *rises in order to hide her emotion;* ALF *follows her and kneels beside her.*

ALF. Only a word for me!

SVAVA. But don't you understand, then, that if you could once more give me the joy that springs from nothing but complete trust—do you think I should be waiting for you then? No, I would come and thank you on my knees!   Can you for a moment doubt that?

ALF. No, no!

SVAVA. But now I don't have it.

ALF. Svava!

SVAVA. Oh, please!

ALF. Good-bye!—Oh, good-bye!—But to meet again!—To meet again! [*He starts to leave but turns back at the door*] I *must* have a sign. A sure sign! Hold out a hand to me!

> SVAVA *turns toward him and holds out both her hands.*
> ALF *goes out.*

MRS. RIIS. [*Comes through the door on the left*] Did you give him any promise?

SVAVA. I think I did!

> [*She hides her face against her mother's shoulder.*

Curtain.